LEADERSHIP BY THE BOOK

INSPIRING OTHERS WITH STORIES OF SUCCESS

TABLE OF CONTENTS

PUBLISHER'S NOTE V

INTRODUCTION VI

BUSINESS

ALL IN: 101 REAL-LIFE BUSINESS LESSONS FOR EMERGING ENTREPRENEURS
BILL GREEN 2

FROM THE GROUND UP
DAN HOFFLER WITH JOE COCCARO 6

WEALTH OF INSIGHT: THE WORLD'S BEST LUXURY HOTELIERS ON LEADERSHIP, MANAGEMENT, AND THE FUTURE OF 5-STAR HOSPITALITY
RAHIM B. KANANI 10

LOVING LIFE: FIVE DECADES IN RADIO AND TV
GENE LOVING WITH JOE COCCARO 14

WOUNDED WARRIOR, WOUNDED WIFE: NOT JUST SURVIVING BUT THRIVING
BARBARA MCNALLY 18

HIDDEN IN PLAIN VIEW: RECOGNIZING THE OBVIOUS— EXPLOITING THE OBSCURE IN FLY FISHING
DUANE REDFORD 22

PAPA: THE STORY OF PAPA JOHN'S PIZZA
JOHN SCHNATTER 26

YOUR BRIDAL STYLE: EVERYTHING YOU NEED TO KNOW TO DESIGN THE WEDDING OF YOUR DREAMS
RANI ST. PUCCHI 30

THINK OUTSIDE THE BOTTLE: THE PRODUCT ENTREPRENEUR'S PLAYBOOK
DUANE THOMPSON WITH CHERYL ROSS . . . 34

UNITED WAY WOMEN OF PHILANTHROPY: 100 WOMEN UNITED 38

HEALTH

LOST AND FOUND: A CONSUMER'S GUIDE TO HEALTHCARE
PETER B. ANDERSON, MD AND
PAUL H. GRUNDY, MD WITH TOM EMSWILLER
AND BUD RAMEY 44

MY FATHER'S GIFT: HOW ONE MAN'S PURPOSE BECAME A
JOURNEY OF HOPE AND HEALING
SIXTUS Z. ATABONG 48

AUTISM UNCENSORED: PULLING BACK THE CURTAIN
WHITNEY ELLENBY 52

THE FALLACY OF THE CALORIE: WHY THE MODERN WESTERN
DIET IS KILLING US AND HOW TO STOP IT
MICHAEL S. FENSTER, MD 56

THE DOCTOR NEXT DOOR
ELAINE HOLT, MD 60

LIFESAVING LABRADORS: TRUE STORIES OF DIABETIC ALERT DOGS
FROM WILDROSE KENNELS
BEN MCCLELAND 64

MEDICAL CANNABIS: A GUIDE FOR PATIENTS, PRACTITIONERS,
AND CAREGIVERS
MICHAEL H. MOSKOWITZ, MD, MPH 68

NEW ADHD MEDICATION RULES: BRAIN SCIENCE & COMMON SENSE
DR. CHARLES PARKER 72

M. GAZI YASARGIL: FATHER OF MODERN NEUROSURGERY
LARRY ROGERS, MD 76

RUNNING IN SILENCE: MY DRIVE FOR PERFECTION AND THE EATING
DISORDER THAT FED IT
RACHAEL ROSE STEIL 80

PERFECT: STORIES FROM THE HEART OF A DAD
JOHN T. WAGNER 84

***A portion of the proceeds from this book will be
donated to The Muse Writers Center***

The Muse is dedicated to broadening community awareness and support of the literary arts. In addition to offering writing classes, The Muse is a resource center and a place for all writers in the Norfolk, Virginia (Hampton Roads, VA) area to come together, share ideas, and figure out what language can hold.

PUBLISHER'S NOTE

Sometimes leaders must retreat in order to succeed. Such was the case with this book. I originally wanted to celebrate our many memoirs and business books written by authors from across many industries, so I set things in motion. My staff and I pulled a list of more than fifty exemplary books published by our company, Koehler Books. We worked hard to craft the concept. I was excited.

We had a strategy session with our core team comprised of myself, Joe Coccaro, Bud Ramey, Kellie Emery and Hannah Woodlan. We discussed the book project, presented our data, brainstormed and tweaked assumptions. We beat up the idea of publishing a celebratory book of business and biographical titles and nearly nixed the idea. Admittedly, I was fuming at the apparent lack of enthusiasm among my colleagues. It seemed like a great idea—my idea—was about to die.

Joe was quiet. Thinking. Then he said, "This is really a leadership book. It's about leaders, and the two primary markets are business and healthcare."

Boom! Everything fell into place. Even though we had all of the components we needed, and had done the preliminary work and organized the data, the whole was not greater than the parts. Joe reshuffled the deck and exposed the way forward and the simple truth.

Leadership is about considering all angles and being willing to pivot and give up on any preconceived notion in favor of finding the best solution. You have to mine the field to find the gold. You have to dim your ego so others can shine. You have to be willing to fail in order to win. Accomplished and successful leaders know this and so much more. Their wisdom is their legacy, which is why I was, and am, so anxious to celebrate their words.

So, it's with great joy that I present *Leadership by the Book*.

—John Koehler
President and publisher, Koehler Books

INTRODUCTION

SHARING YOUR SUCCESS:

Why leaders should tell their stories

> " LEADERSHIP IS NOT ABOUT TITLES, POSITIONS, OR FLOW CHARTS. IT IS ABOUT ONE LIFE INFLUENCING ANOTHER. "

—John C. Maxwell

From our earliest days, humans are taught to follow. We learn almost immediately to obey rules and mimic acceptable behaviors. We are, at our essence, copycats; we model the success of others—or at least we try—and attempt to dodge failure.

Growing up, we inevitably want to be "like" someone we admire. "I want to be like Mike!" Remember that from Michael Jordan's heyday? The sports world is rife with athletic icons who inspire others to either admire or attempt greatness. Non-jocks might hero-worship a great painter, writer, or technological innovator, such as Apple founder Steve Jobs. For physicists it might be Stephen Hawking; for law students Sonia Sotomayor; for investors Warren Buffet; for actors Denzel Washington; for military strategists Admiral Chester Nimitz. You get the idea. These are universal figures, the biggest fish in the largest oceans.

More likely, the people we aspire to become reside in an office down the hall, or nearby in a laboratory or hospital. They lead the organization we work for or patronize. They're the entrepreneurs, CEOs, MDs, CPAs, engineers, developers, architects who have led great companies or have made watershed discoveries. They employ and heal us; they're bread-and-butter heroes of our lake-sized communities.

The successes of these leaders inspire others. They are our role models, those who set standards of excellence. We learn from them right from wrong, when to relent or be relentless, how to persevere, or when to adapt. We learn whose behavior they modeled, who or what they feared most, and who inspired them. Leaders writing about other leaders maintains the thread of success.

The question invariably becomes not what someone achieved, but how. We know that Steve Jobs co-founded Apple Inc. and that the company revolutionized our world with technology. The 2011 biography about Jobs garnered huge commercial success because Apple geeks and millions of others clamored to know what motivated the man to greatness.

Unfortunately, the legacy for most great achievers is only *what* they accomplished. More valuable is the *how*, or *why*. When that leader moves on or retires, the wisdom exists only in shreds and, over time, that brilliance dims. "Old soldiers never die; they just fade away." Remember that quote from General MacArthur? I always found it depressing. Great leaders should be remembered and studied instead of vanishing into the fog of time. Otherwise, too much learning is lost. MacArthur had a huge footprint and his legacy lives in countless books and museums, but his point is well taken. Most just fade into the shadows.

One of the most gratifying aspects of our work at Koehler Books has been working with dozens of business and health care leaders to preserve for perpetuity the *hows* and *whys* of their successes. Each has come to the table humble, or even slightly embarrassed, about sharing his story, some feeling more vain than instructive. In nearly every case, we have found their stories to be inspiring, and more than worthy of preservation. Most of all, we've been surprised by their depth and substance.

People confuse luck and success. Too often I have heard that someone succeeded because he got "lucky." When you drill down into Mr. Lucky's story, what you more often find is that he positioned himself to capitalize on luck, should that magical pixie dust ever find him. There's also another common element called hard work. The most successful men and women we have published worked relentlessly and stayed focused—even single-minded. Still others were perpetually optimistic, suffocating negativity with visions of success.

We recently published a book that contained essays on leadership written by the general managers of the top luxury hotels around the world. Many of the GMs started meagerly and worked their way up. All espoused hard work, tireless dedication to customers, and hiring well as their recipe for success. There was more learning and wisdom about the hotel business in that one book than a library full of management texts in business schools.

Such learning is a valuable resource, just like precious metals. It should be mined, preserved and then put to use. Leaving the *hows* and *whys* of success buried in a dark hole is not only a waste, it's a disservice to others. How can we mimic success unless we see it? Gold buried in the ground is worthless until extracted.

Sharing success—and the warts of failure—is a gift to others. It's not bragging about wealth or accomplishment. In fact, I would proffer that it's selfish not to share success. You owe it to the people who played support roles in your professional life, to the people filling your footsteps or being groomed to do so, and the generations to come who could benefit by seeing and hearing from your methods and vision.

If you write a book, or have one written about your company, or your research, or your wins and losses, you do so for others—not yourself. Your ego will die with you, but your life's work will continue through the narrative you put to paper. It's simply a way of giving something back, a "thank you" and hand up to those who have admired you, and others curious about your ascension. Being candid about what you know and have experienced can improve your industry or company and that, in turn, makes for a better society. That's what I mean by giving something back.

We take pride in every book we edit, design and publish at Koehler Books. *Every* book and genre are important to us. But we feel particularly fulfilled to assist accomplished leaders with their stories. It's our small way of giving back, too.

The following pages contain examples of some of the many memoirs and other works we have published by leaders. A few of the selections are stories of inspiration or triumph over tragedy. Others exemplify books as a marketing tool or brand extension. Titles like these are powerful calling cards that bring recognition. And, like memoirs, they inspire with stories of success and struggles.

We hope that the following pages, at very least, tempt you to capture for posterity your incredible life of learning, and the *hows* and *whys* that made your life notable. Doing so will be more of a legacy than a name on a building. Your story will provide context for your success, and a compass for those attempting to follow your path.

Assuming all the lights turn green and a leader climbs on board the proverbial Book Train, the question switches from "why" do a book to "how." How do you go about writing your book? Are you capable of writing it yourself or do you need to get professional help? What role will you play in the promotion and marketing of your book? What are your goals for your book?

Some of the leaders we have worked with already have their manuscript written. They come to us, like any other authors, to turn their work into something highly polished and attractive, and then to release it to the world. Discussion inevitably flips from the creative processes of writing, editing and book design, to distributing and marketing. Our mission is to facilitate the process using Ingram, the largest book printer and distributor in the world. We were named outstanding publisher for 2017 by a division of the company called IngramSpark because of our business ethics and practices.

A few years ago we created the Koehler Books Emerging Authors Program for talented debut writers and accomplished leaders. Nearly every book showcased here was born through that program. It's a collaborative publishing model whereby Koehler Books and the authors share some of the expense of publishing and work closely on the book's design and creative development. It's truly a partnership.

When it comes to creating a manuscript, some are do-it-yourselfers who write the bulk of the material. Others hire what we call "ghost writers," who do virtually all of the interviewing, research and writing for a leader. Some leaders opt to co-author with a writing professional. As executive editor, I have co-authored some books, ghostwritten others and worked extensively with many do-it-yourselfers to shape and hone their story. There is no formula. The best publishers provide whatever writers need to fully develop their stories.

Regardless of how we receive a finished manuscript—whether ghostwritten, or written entirely by the author, or something in between—

the process shifts to transforming the draft manuscript into a finished book. We review author submissions and offer our honest assessment of the work, evaluating how much rewriting or editing it might need, design options and how best to distribute and market the work. After discussions with the author, assuming both parties agree there is a good fit, we offer a publishing contract, which typically includes editing, proofreading, cover design, interior layout and marketing strategy sessions.

Most of the leaders we have worked with are committed to doing their part on the publishing team, and agree to follow our lead during the journey. A willingness to collaborate is critical, and good leaders almost always embrace the opportunity to work shoulder to shoulder with us. From cover design to editing and layout, the author is part of a process that can be demanding at times, fun, and rewarding.

Aside from their actual stories, we have found that our leader-authors excel at marketing and promoting—or they employ others with the expertise. We help them apply that knowledge to their book, and teach them the best strategies for getting the word out. Some leaders hire a publicist, others send out hundreds of books to influencers, or plan a book tour across the country, or run ads in periodicals. We help authors tailor a program that makes sense for their book and goals.

Many of our leaders use their books to promote their company, or brand, or nonprofit efforts. They give their books away to business prospects, employees, donors, family and friends. They leverage their book as a door opener, a business card, the perfect leave-behind. Others opt for large commercial sales, ginning up publicity and funding marketing campaigns.

The mechanics of book publishing and distribution can be daunting. There are lots of choices and strategies. What's paramount, however, is that each author start with an excellent book—one that is superbly written, edited and designed. You can have the loudest and most whiz-bang marketing plan, but if your book is shoddy, no one will buy it, and few will admire it. Lousy books live as long as good ones.

Our advice, whether you publish with Koehler Books or not, is to do it right. Don't skimp. Hire or work with professionals you trust and with a proven track record of writing, editing and producing high caliber works.

Thank you for taking the time to consider our words. We hope that the books showcased here, which are just a few of the many we have published, will inspire you to share your story with us.

Warm regards,

Joe Coccaro
Executive editor

BUSINESS

ALL IN
101 REAL-LIFE BUSINESS LESSONS FOR EMERGING ENTREPRENEURS

by Bill Green

PAGES: 252

PUB DATE: 06-15-2017

SOFTCOVER: $17.95 978-1-63393-464-1

HARDCOVER: $25.95 978-1-63393-466-5

EBOOK: $9.99 978-1-63393-465-8

> "Bill Green's inspiring *All In, 101 Real-Life Lessons* is not a book! It is the personal and intimate conversation between you, the reader, and the author, who shares one of the most amazing and motivating journeys to success."
>
> –DWIGHT CAREY, CEO American Productivity Group and Asst. Prof. of Entrepreneurship Temple University

ABOUT THE BOOK

You have the Big Idea, the drive and ambition. You see the market, and you've identified the customers. You want to be wildly successful. You wonder how certain entrepreneurs have achieved success without a fancy education or unlimited access to capital. Enter Bill Green, a serial entrepreneur. Using his own impressive business achievements (and his few fiascos), Green provides the reader with the practical tools needed to launch their Big Idea or improve their existing business. In a unique, humorous, and impassioned style, Bill shares 101 key insights he has gleaned over a forty-year business career that began with a single flea market table. He shares the lessons he learned that allowed him to leverage his flea market business table into one of the largest industrial distribution companies in the country and how he subsequently successfully invested in or founded numerous companies across multiple end markets. His message is universal and is the ideal road map for anyone who might wonder how the Bill Greens of the business world do what they do so well.

ABOUT THE AUTHOR

Bill Green is an author, and the founder and CEO of the Crestar Group of Companies. Crestar is comprised of private equity, specialty finance, and real estate businesses. Bill is also the CEO of LendingOne, which was founded in 2014. LendingOne provides real estate bridge and rental loans for non-owner-occupied real estate investors properties. Prior to forming Crestar, Mr. Green was with Interline Brands, founding the company in 1977. For twenty-five years he led Interline as its CEO from a small retail outlet to one of the largest industrial distribution companies in the country. Today, Interline Brands is owned by Home Depot. Bill is a member of Young Presidents Organization and has served on numerous nonprofit boards over the years. Currently, he serves on the Foundation Board of Trustees for the Children's Hospital of Philadelphia.

I was once you.

I will admit, I'm a sentimental guy. Growing up in the New Jersey suburbs the way I did, I wasn't born with a silver spoon in my mouth. I didn't come from a wealthy family. I certainly never went on any fancy vacations or attended any highbrow boarding schools. In fact, I never even graduated from college.

Heck, I barely graduated from high school! I was too busy building a business as a teenager to bother too much with homework or science projects. I'm what you call an "old-school" self-made man. No one gave me anything in life; I got my education in the real world where grades really counted—and boy, am I glad I did, because the insights I gained while "just doing it" have lasted me a lifetime.

My humble background is why I'll always have a soft spot in my heart for feisty entrepreneurs like you. Forty years ago, I was you. I was a small business owner who had a great idea for a business that I brought to life, and it was chugging along pretty well. I shouldn't have had any complaints. I was living the dream. But you know what? I had that same itch you do.

I didn't want to settle for good; I wanted great. Not just great, I wanted amazing. I didn't want to beat my competition. I wanted to own them.

Maybe you haven't been given anything. Maybe you didn't draw the luckiest lot in life. Neither did I. What's behind you is not important. No one will remember where you started. They'll only remember where you finish. Your dreams may seem like a fantasy to most people now, but if you combine a great idea with a lot of persistent and consistent hard work, you can get anything you want out of life.

Just look at me. I did it and along the way I learned 101 essential insights into making your business great that can be applied to virtually any business model on earth. These are the lessons I'm going to share with you. I didn't just wake up one day and have all these epiphanies. All these things I learned from experience. I had to make mistakes, I had to try again, I had to keep coming back day after day until I got it right. I don't want you to make the same mistakes I did.

This book is a hybrid. I'm going to tell you my own story, not to gratify my ego, but because there are a lot of things I went through that might be useful for you to learn from.

In addition, I'm distilling some of the key learning experiences into those 101 essential insights I mentioned a moment earlier. I hope you draw inspiration from my story, and I hope you take to heart the lessons I share.

If you've got the same drive I do, and I know you do, I want to show you how to conceive, build, and grow your business from a neophyte startup into a market-dominating company that provides amazing service, employs talented and motivated people, and attracts customers who don't just like you—they love you. They need you. They can't live without you.

Sound like fun? Sure it does!

FEATURED AUTHOR Q&A:

What inspired you to write your manuscript?

My success story is pretty cool, but I never planned to write a book about it. My dad was diagnosed with Alzheimer's disease, asking me the same questions over and over again. I began to worry that the same thing would eventually happen to me. I wanted to insure that my kids and grandchildren knew the details of my life story with all of its crazy twists and turns, successes and mistakes. So I started writing and when I thought I had a good outline I locked myself in a hotel room in Florida for 3 days and dictated my story and my most important business lessons into my iPhone. I sent the recording to a transcriptionist and it turned out to be 375 pages. After some professionally editing i felt i had a great keepsake for my family. But then I shared it with a friend who said "Bill—this is a book—a really good one!" That is how my book came to be. I think of "all in" as a road map that shares my scrappy street smarts with the world and with emerging entrepreneurs like yourselves.

Describe your book in one sentence.

I think of *All In* as a road map that shares my scrappy street smarts with the world and with aspiring and emerging entrepreneurs.

What is your number one piece of advice to an aspiring writer/entrepreneur?

To aspiring entrepreneurs—Read my book!

Are you currently writing anything else?

I am currently writing a weekly article for Inc.com, although I do plan on writing a second book within the next couple of years.

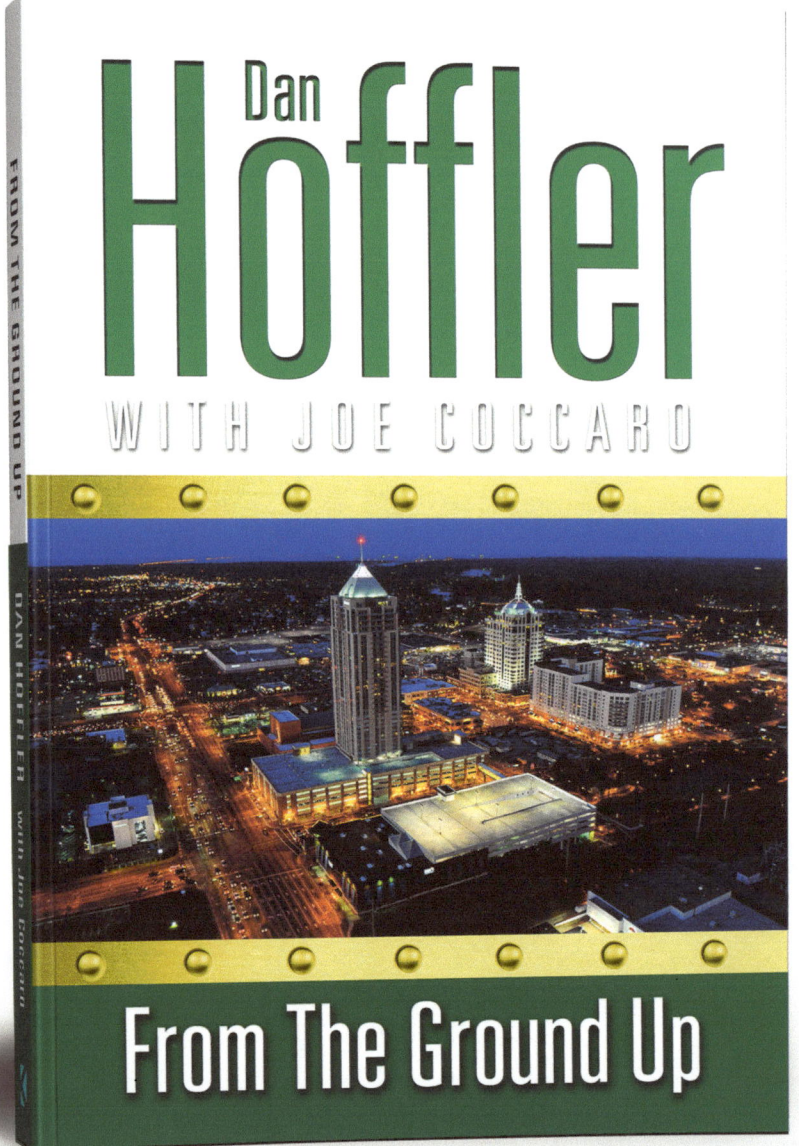

FROM THE GROUND UP

by Dan Hoffler
with Joe Coccaro

PAGES: 200

PUB DATE: 04-01-2013

SOFTCOVER: $14.95 978-1-938467-44-8

HARDCOVER: $26.95 978-1-938467-53-0

EBOOK: $7.99 978-1-938467-78-3

> "Dan values family very highly. A lot of the respect that he has on a personal level carries forward in business... Everyone needs someone to talk to, and I trusted him implicitly."
>
> — L. DOUGLAS WILDER, former Virginia governor

ABOUT THE BOOK

From the Ground Up is the journey of real estate magnate Dan Hoffler, a person from a very modest family, a kid with average grades and a big smile, who succeeded in business on the force of personality and a strong belief in himself.

Hoffler's story is rife with life lessons on finding success, coping with controversy, and always enjoying life. He is a world traveler and big game hunter who tells of his harrowing pursuit of polar bear, rhino, and mountain sheep in some of the most remote and dangerous regions in the world. The book includes anecdotes from NFL Hall-of-Famer Bruce Smith, US Senator Mark Warner and former Virginia governor Doug Wilder.

ABOUT THE AUTHOR

Dan Hoffler is a commercial real estate magnate whose Virginia Beach, Virginia, company, Armada Hoffler, has built marquee office towers, hotels, and retail hubs in major cities along the East Coast. He is an outdoor enthusiast and marksman who has hunted big game on five continents. A graduate of Campbell University in North Carolina, Dan has served as a director on several state and private boards, including the Shaw Group, a Fortune 500 company. Dan has four children and lives on Virginia's Eastern Shore with his wife, Valerie.

Dad wanted to show me where he worked. Until now, his job had been somewhat of a mystery. I remember Mom dropping off Dad at work on occasion. I'd be in the car, gazing at the shipyard and thinking that it looked endless. Massive ships in dry dock on the water's edge with their great hulls were taller than any building I had ever seen. Some had big white numbers, meaning they were warships.

Parking lots the size of football fields were packed with pick-ups and Chevys. Workers changing shifts filed in and out of the entrance gates like bees to a hive in the spring.

Dad stood out from most men entering and exiting. He wore a white shirt and tie, a fact my mother was always proud of. Dad was a draftsman, an office worker. Most others were welders, pipefitters, electricians, laborers, painters or sandblasters. They donned overalls or jeans, sweatshirts and ball caps. They had beards, rough hands, smoked cigarettes, ate ham sandwiches and drank coffee from a thermos. The tint of their work clothes was much like the shipyard itself: lots of dark blues, grays and browns. Nowhere was Portsmouth, Virginia's lineage as a blue-collar town more apparent.

It was on a Saturday morning after breakfast that Dad took me for the visit. I was about age five.

I stood a few steps behind Dad as we approached an entrance gate. Dad spoke briefly and quietly to a security guard. I don't remember exactly what the man said to my father, but I am clear about the way Dad was treated.

My dad, Alfred Hoffler, was then as he always has been, gentle and soft-spoken, with soft blue eyes and an easy smile. Not once as a boy or later in life did my father raise his voice at me, my sister, and certainly not my mother, Sarah. He rarely showed disappointment or frustration and never displayed anger. He showed the same restraint and civility on the morning of our visit to the shipyard.

The guard was smug and condescending. He clearly didn't want to let us into the yard. I remember my father being embarrassed, saying only that he wanted to show his son where he worked, that we wouldn't be roaming around the yard itself, only his office. Others had been allowed to bring kin to work.

The guard insulted my father and, even worse, marginalized a man in front of his son. He made my father grovel for no apparent reason other than to demonstrate his own authority. My father was not so important that the guard would just let him enter unquestioned. The guard could, if he wanted, turn my father away.

I remained silent, trying at first to understand what was happening, and then, why. Anger came next and then a lesson that imprinted me forever. I decided at that moment that I never wanted to be treated with such disrespect; I never wanted to be so beholden to another person or job that a boss, coworker or security guard could humiliate me without consequence. I never wanted to be that callous or insensitive to others, seeing the hurt on my dad's face. For me, the revelation was about showing decency to others and expecting the same in return. Never since that day have I seen the upside in being disrespectful or demeaning—to anyone. After our visit that day, I left determined that no one would douse my self-esteem.

My father's temperament and my mother's unrelenting encouragement provided the foundation for my life as a father businessman and adventurer. I owe them everything, and perhaps more importantly, I admire them deeply. They are my heroes.

There were no silver spoons in my young life, but there were lots of silver linings. Alfred and Sarah Hoffler taught me to believe in myself, not settle for less, and to aim high. I listened to them, and because of their lessons things usually turned out well for me, even if they started off shaky. I am not sure what to call it—fate, luck, karma, divine intervention? More than once I have made spontaneous decisions for reasons I still do not fully understand. These choices either enabled me to avert financial disaster or to profit tremendously. In business, timing isn't everything, but it can be hugely important. I have also been a student of human behavior. My mentor, a Texas oilman named Jim Fisher, taught me to "trust my gut." That's been especially important when sorting out whom to do business with.

I decided to chronicle my life's journey with the hope that my family, supporters, coworkers and others will learn from my fits and starts. I hope to inspire others who come from common backgrounds such as mine. I hope my story shows that if you believe in yourself, others will believe in you. As for those who do not, forget about them. I have found most of my detractors to be envious, petty or political.

This book is also a tribute to my parents and the core group of partners and friends who believed in me and remained loyal through three recessions, three marriages, a few mistakes and some bad press. My wife, Valerie, and my children have also been loving and stable forces in my life.

I have been fortunate, more fortunate than most, to have such dedicated partners and family to lean on. My deepest gratitude goes to my lifelong friend and right-hand man, Russ Kirk, and the gifted executive who runs the day-to-day affairs of our development and construction businesses, Louis Haddad. With these men at the helm, my company, Armada Hoffler, has built some of the grandest hotels, office buildings and industrial parks on the East Coast. Our buildings fill the skylines of Virginia Beach, Norfolk, Washington and Baltimore. When I see these trophies in the sky, I think of Russ, Lou and the dedicated staff who helped shape Armada Hoffler over three decades.

Through our dealings I have come to know others with money and influence. Friends include CEOs of Fortune 500 companies, NASCAR drivers, NFL stars, U.S. senators, mayors, Virginia governors, Navy admirals and famous entertainers. Successful people often travel the same orbits. It's natural that they form bonds that sometimes sprout into friendships. Deals do get made over drinks, private dinners and while on exotic trips. But they're initiated on trust and built upon a bedrock of integrity.

Among those dearest to me are people most like my parents, honest folks with average incomes toiling to be providers and to do right by others. I often find "regular" people—some of them farmers, tradesmen, secretaries, hunting guides, real estate agents and restaurant staffers—even more extraordinary than those with big titles and several homes. Integrity, I have found, is a common denominator for success in all of us. People without it are often not true to themselves, which makes it impossible to be true to others. Avoid them in business and in life.

You'll find in these pages that I don't pretend to be some kind of business apostle or moralist or tech-savvy trailblazer. My success has come from the tried-and-true formula of hard work and salesmanship. I am a "people" guy, an extrovert who likes getting to know folks and being around others who enjoy life. I see the possibilities in people and business deals and try to match the two. You might say I am a capitalistic Cupid.

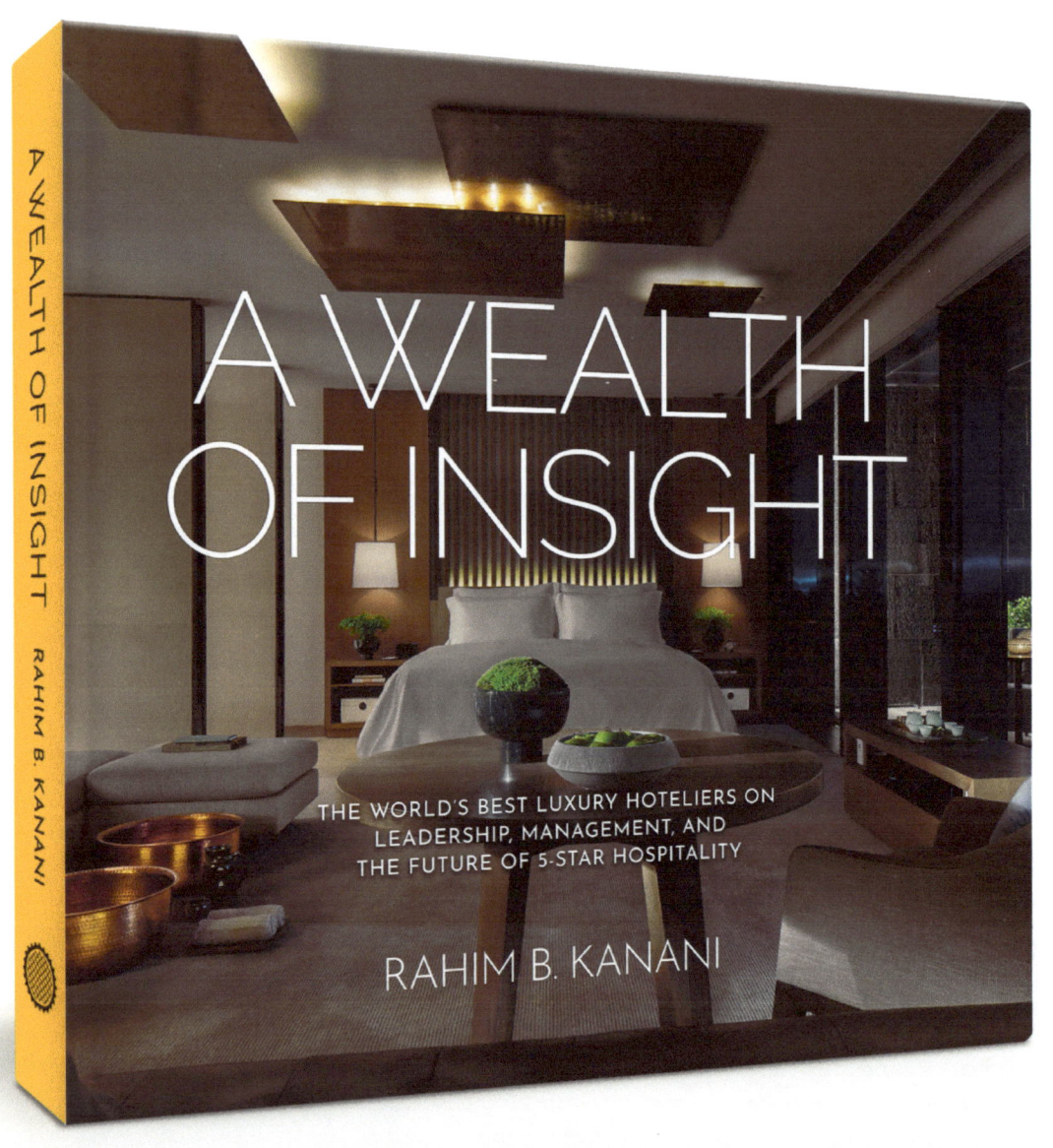

A WEALTH OF INSIGHT

THE WORLD'S BEST LUXURY HOTELIERS ON LEADERSHIP, MANAGEMENT, AND THE FUTURE OF 5-STAR HOSPITATLITY

by Rahim B. Kanani

PAGES: 354

PUB DATE: 12-15-2017

HARDCOVER: $39.95, 978-1-63393-620-1

EBOOK: $9.99, 978-1-63393-621-8

SELF PUBLISHED BY BLACK TRUFFLE PRESS

" . . . an enlightening read, intelligently written, and comprehensive in its reflection, culminating in an impressive, long-overdue publication of this nature and magnitude."

—DR. DIMITRIOS DIAMANTIS, dean of Graduate Studies, Les Roches, Global Hospitality Education, Switzerland

ABOUT THE BOOK

In *A Wealth of Insight*, more than thirty-five of the world's best luxury hoteliers share exactly what it takes to lead and manage some of the most legendary hotels and resorts. Each executive profile includes bite-size insights, stunning photography and real-life examples on recruiting, culture, technology, marketing, branding, personalization, authenticity, anticipation, design, partnerships and more. Hoteliers also detail the most significant trends impacting the sector today, and how those trends will shape the future of luxury hospitality. The sheer scale and scope of this effort—to distill industry wisdom across two dozen countries—is unprecedented.

For aspiring and current general managers of luxury hotels, for hospitality executives in search of a practical guide on how best to deliver a world-class guest experience, and for the modern luxury traveler eager to go behind the scenes, *A Wealth of Insight* is the holy grail of five-star leadership and management.

ABOUT THE AUTHOR

Rahim B. Kanani is a leadership, luxury, and travel contributor to a number of global publications, including *Forbes Middle East* and *Black Truffle Club.* Over the years, he has interviewed more than 500 of the world's most innovative, influential, and award-winning executives on leadership, management, and creativity. Notable interviewees have included billionaires Jeff Skoll, Michael Bloomberg, Tory Burch and Eli Broad, world-renowned chefs Eric Ripert, Daniel Humm, José Andrés, and Anthony Bourdain, musical artists Alicia Keys, Madonna, and Shakira, Hollywood filmmaker James Cameron, Harvard University president Drew Faust, former British prime minister Tony Blair, and Princess Ameerah Al-Taweel of Saudi Arabia. During this time, he served as a leadership contributor to *Forbes* and *Thomson Reuters Foundation*, while also authoring or editing articles and interviews published in *Harvard Business Review, CNN Opinion, Financial Times, Fast Company, Food & Wine,* and others.

While pursuing an undergraduate degree in philosophy many years ago, I developed a hunger for knowledge—not for facts and figures, but for perennial wisdom and insight. Fueled by intense curiosity, a passion for conversation, and a desire to discover the world, I spent nearly a decade distilling leadership and management insights from some of the most innovative and influential chief executives across industries. As I traversed the globe from San Francisco to Stockholm to Seoul, I often laid rest at a world-class hotel befitting of my interviewees. In fact, many discussions took place in glamorous suites, lobbies, and ballrooms.

Over the years, the luxury hotel—symbolic of my travels and journalism—shifted from stage to spotlight. From the moment I arrived, every aspect of the guest experience was carefully crafted, catering to all five senses. It was awe-inspiring, delightful and flawless. I became obsessed with how such properties balanced intuitive care with military precision, so I turned my attention to pulling back the curtain and uncovering the secret to creating a world-class guest experience. To do this project justice, I needed to interview the tip of the spear—general managers who have spent decades on the frontlines, rising the ranks and ultimately stewarding some of the world's most luxurious hotels and resorts. Almost a year from the moment I decided to embark on this journey, I am honored and humbled to say that I've done exactly that.

More than thirty-five of the world's best luxury hoteliers participated in this special effort, contributing many hours of their time and sharing many decades of their experience. Every hotelier profile includes bite-size insights, stunning photography and real-life examples on recruiting, culture, technology, marketing, branding, personalization, authenticity, anticipation, design, partnerships and more. Their contributions represent the spectrum of a luxury hotelier's mindshare.

Today, general managers are adapting their design and service offerings to meet the needs of a new generation of modern luxury travelers who prize authenticity over familiarity, simplicity over complexity, exclusive experiences over champagne and caviar, and insider knowledge over high-end shopping—hallmarks of becoming a serious destination authority. In addition, luxury hoteliers now operate in a much more dynamic and immediate environment—working closely with investors as owners to meet expectations of financial performance, monitoring digital platforms to rapidly react to guest feedback, and constantly innovating to differentiate themselves in hyper-competitive markets.

While the very definition of luxury has changed, and the environment in which general managers operate has become increasingly complex, core leadership and management principles underpinning the industry remain intact.

Every hotelier featured in this book exudes a fundamental understanding of genuine human connection. They reveal a mastery in the art and science of recruiting, developing, motivating and managing a world-class team—explicitly designed to deliver on the promise of personalized luxury at every stage of the guest experience. This is one of the most profound insights to emerge from this endeavor. The most beautiful of hotels in the most coveted of locations cannot deliver on that promise without an extraordinarily passionate and talented team committed to perfection. There is no alternative. In an industry that now Googles guests in advance of their stay to glean personal and professional interests, likes and dislikes, anticipatory service is not simply possessing information, but acting on it deliberately, thoughtfully and discreetly.

For aspiring and current general managers of luxury hotels around the world, for hospitality executives in search of a practical guide on how best to deliver a world-class guest experience, and for the modern luxury traveler eager to go behind the scenes, *A Wealth of Insight* is the holy grail of five-star leadership and management.

The search for wisdom continues.

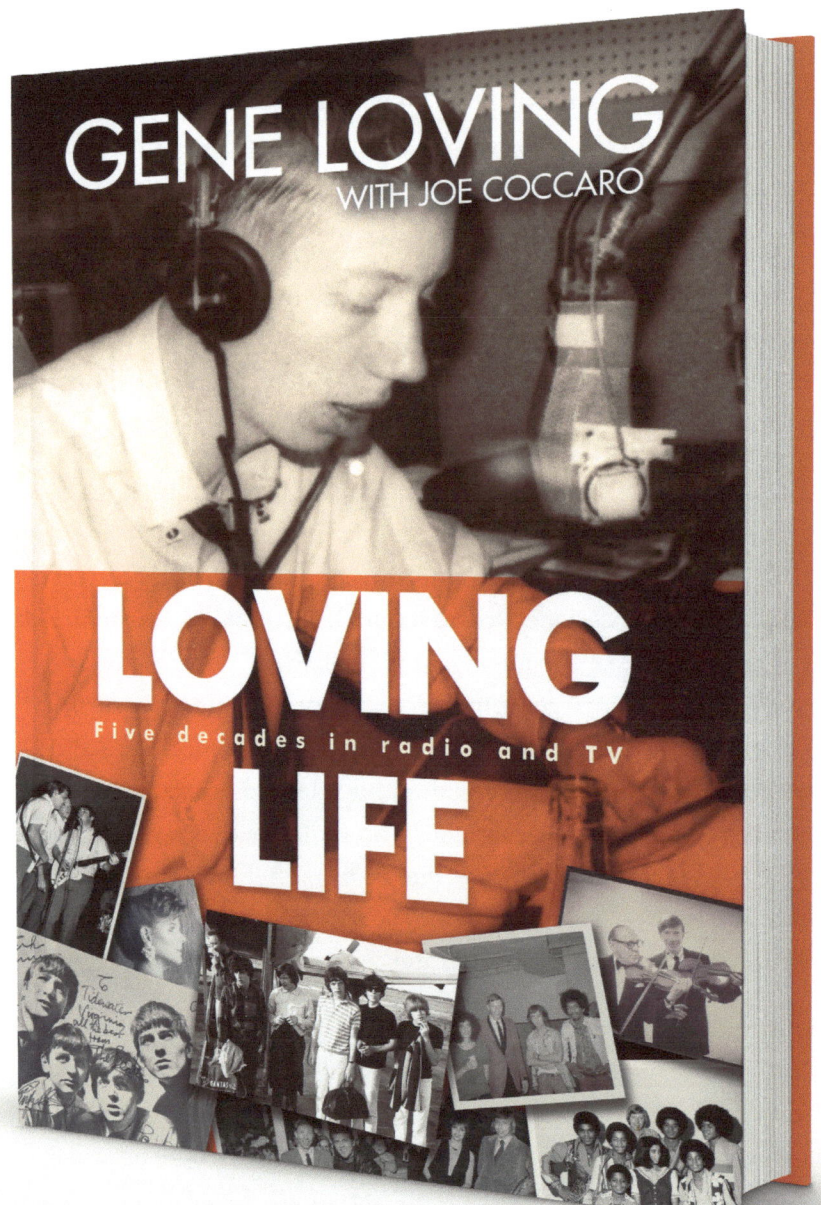

LOVING LIFE
FIVE DECADES IN RADIO AND TV

by Gene Loving
with Joe Coccaro

PAGES: 406

PUB DATE: 02-22-2018

SOFTCOVER: $32.95 978-1-63393-272-2

HARDCOVER: $49.95 978-1-63393-274-6

EBOOK: $9.99 978-1-63393-273-9

ABOUT THE BOOK

The tall, skinny kid with a deep voice and a small record collection launched his first radio station even before starting high school. He would over the next four decades become one of Virginia's most recognized on-air personalities, concert promoters and media trailblazers. Gene Loving was the first DJ in the country to pick a Beatles record as a future hit and accompany the band to its inaugural US concert. He rode the tidal wave of rock and roll throughout the 1960s, hanging out backstage with the biggest names in the business: Jimi Hendrix, The Rolling Stones, The Beach Boys, Sonny and Cher, James Brown, to name a few.

Gene was a radio and television visionary, starting one of the largest chains of independent TV stations in US history. His on-air persona and behind-the-scenes business dealings are part of the fabric of America's music and entertainment story. In his memoir, *Loving Life*, Gene shares his exploits in vivid detail, giving readers a front-row seat to a slice of Americana.

ABOUT THE AUTHOR

Gene Loving began his career as an on-air personality in his hometown of Richmond, Virginia in 1958. During the early 1960s his interviews with the Beatles were syndicated across the United States and other countries. Loving also co-founded Max Media Properties, which was sold to publicly traded Sinclair of Baltimore in 1998. Gene started TVX Broadcast Group, which was later sold to Paramount Pictures in 1991, and also founded and developed Hampton Roads Wireless. He has received prestigious awards and recognition from broadcast and advertising trade associations. He is also a director on the board of New Dominion Pictures, following similar positions at ATO Pictures, Metro Information Services, and Monarch Bank. Gene is a former director of Operation Smile, an international children's health organization, and served on the boards of Sentara Health Care and the Virginia Marine Science Museum. He has been a member of various committees of Spring Branch Community Church. Loving is currently chairman and CEO of Max Media LLC, a Virginia Beach company that owns and operates television, radio, and alternative media. He resides in Virginia Beach with his wife, Angela, and two Shih Tzu dogs, Bella and Cuddles.

I don't know exactly why I liked the song, *She Loves You*, when I first heard it. Maybe it was the simplicity of the lyrics; maybe it was the harmony of the four young Brits singing and playing electric guitars to a steady backbeat. All I knew at the time was that I liked the sound, and that it was different. When you're a DJ in his early 20s and you're paid to pick winners, you had better have good musical instincts. At the time, it's about all you had to go on. So, I went with my gut and chose that catchy tune as my featured record of the day.

It was September 1963, and I was the first DJ in the country to report *She Loves You* as a potential hit following its release in the US by Swan Records. I liked the band so much that I booked them to perform at a 2,000-seat venue in Virginia Beach. To my chagrin, and Swan's, the song went absolutely nowhere—a total flop. Five months later we would be vindicated, in a big way. The lads from Liverpool, with their Edwardian suits and strange haircuts, appeared on *The Ed Sullivan Show*. They performed *She Loves You* " "yeah, yeah, yeah" at the end of their first set in front of screaming teens in the live audience and 73 million people watching from home. That performance triggered a musical tsunami that helped launch the most storied rock 'n' roll band of all time. Being the first to pick *She Loves You* in a national trade paper as a future hit, and later book that group before they were big, gave me entrée to the Beatles when their fame erupted. They wound up canceling the Virginia Beach gig, as their manager decided to abandon the whole spring 1964 tour. But being among the first, if not *the* first, in the US to discover this band put me on the map with the group's US agent, and that relationship ultimately kicked open other doors of opportunity. That success taught me, very early in my career, that timing in show business was, in fact, a springboard to bigger possibilities. And who you know certainly does matter. As I look back on that good fortune now, it's clear I was the right age, in the right market, and on the ground floor at a pivotal time in rock 'n' roll history.

I have spent five decades evolving with the music business, first as a DJ and promoter during the golden days of Top 40 radio, then as a founder and executive of broadcast corporations. I've been a principal owner and operator of radio stations all over the US and founded a company that became the nation's largest group of independent TV stations. My life has been, and continues to be, a whirlwind of meetings, phone calls, logistics and connections.

I got hooked on music as a young boy growing up in central Virginia. With encouragement and support from my parents, I simply followed my passion, forgoing more sensible careers. Along the way, I have accumulated hundreds of stories involving big-name celebrities or those kingmakers handling marquee performers. I've been backstage with John, Paul, George and Ringo, and countless others as they made their fame: Mick Jagger, Jimi Hendrix, Cher, Muhammad Ali, Jack Benny, Dick Clark, Norman Lear, James Brown, The Beach Boys, The Temptations, Three Dog Night.... It's a very long list. I even managed a band—Bill Deal and the Rhondels.

Oftentimes my wife, Angie, or close friends prod me to share some of my wistful moments chauffeuring around big stars, or hanging out with them backstage or taking them to dinner. I have just as many stories about co-workers and investors who helped build significant businesses in radio and TV. On occasion, I oblige Angie (and others who nag me) with a story or two, and every once in a while I even show pictures.

Telling stories and name-dropping to entertain family members, business associates and friends is one thing; having the gumption and the resources to chronicle them in a book is quite another. I would have been happy to keep all of this within the family. But my lovely wife—my unrelenting lovely wife—pushed me hard to share. Angie shamed me by first asking that I do a book just for her, and said it was the only gift she wanted from me for many Christmases to come. Next, she enlisted friends to join the chorus and then found a publisher to be her accomplice. I finally ran out of excuses.

Except for saying "My radio show ratings were always higher than yours," in never-ending arguments with my longtime friend and partner, Dick Lamb, I have tried to avoid glorifying my accomplishments, believing that only *today* and the future are important. I still believe that. But I'm at least willing to admit that some may find use for, or interest in, my professional travails. In many ways, what I experienced is bigger than me. One of the reasons I capitulated and did this book was to chronicle Virginia's broadcast history in the second half of the twentieth century, especially in eastern Virginia. Peter Easter, Executive Director of the Virginia Association of Broadcasters, says I have archived more success in over-the-air radio and TV than any other Virginian, or any other pure broadcast company headquartered in the state. Other Virginia families have founded and built major diversified communications companies and headquartered here, but those riches grew out of the newspaper business—Landmark Communications in Norfolk, Media General in Richmond, and the *Daily Press* in Newport News are among four or five big ones. My roots have always been in broadcast.

My earliest years were as a radio DJ and after that, TV show host. Then I became an owner of radio stations, getting in on the ground floor of the exploding popularity of FM radio. Television station ownership came next. My colleagues and I were among the first big investors in UHF-TV and we grew a company that became the largest chain of independently owned TV stations in the country. I'm still amazed by this success. Statistically, it shouldn't have happened. I started out with empty pockets on the lowest rung of the broadcasting ladder. I ascended a pretty fair distance, risking all my own money while relying on connections to raise the rest. My only inheritance was my parents' support, good nature and strong moral compass.

I have pictures hanging in my office that reflect certain periods in my life—handshakes and hugs with stars, media honchos, and politicians. These photos memorialize, in a small way, some of my good fortune. But I have taken equal pride in aspects of my life outside the office. I have believed that everyone needs a personal life and other interests to provide balance and perspective to your time on earth: the way one earns a living is just one part of who he is.

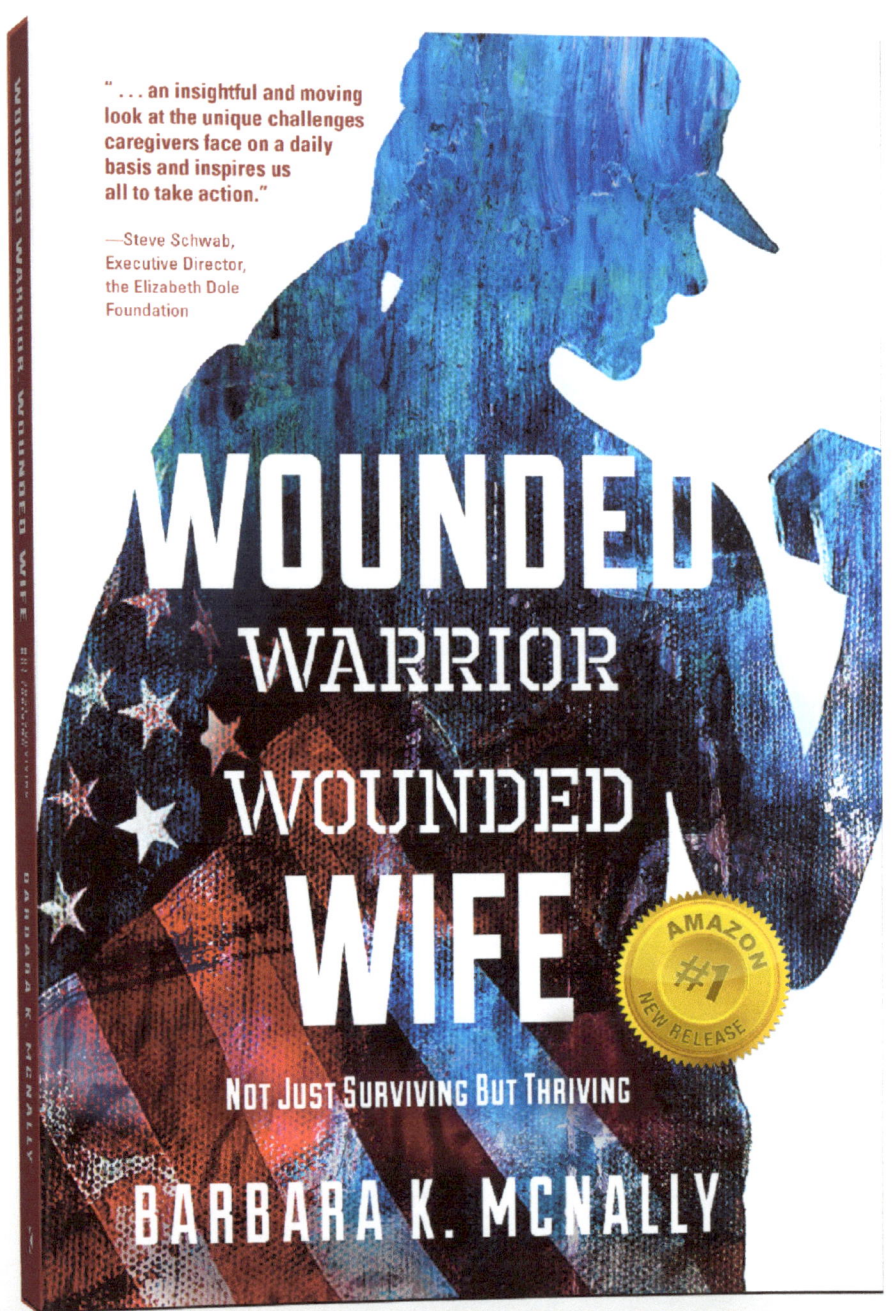

WOUNDED WARRIOR, WOUNDED WIFE

NOT JUST SURVIVING BUT THRIVING

by Barbara K. McNally

PAGES: 228

PUB DATE: 10-15-2016

SOFTCOVER: $14.95 978-1-63393-287-6

HARDCOVER: $24.95 978-1-63393-289-0

EBOOK: $4.99 978-1-63393-288-3

> "... an insightful and moving look at the unique challenges caregivers face on a daily basis and inspires us all to take action."
>
> —STEVE SCHWAB, Executive Director, the Elizabeth Dole Foundation

ABOUT THE BOOK

Imagine sending your spouse to war with a heavy heart, then receiving a life-shattering phone call telling you he's been badly injured. Your beloved returns to your arms, but changed, broken, angry, conflicted, and in need of around-the-clock care. What do you do?

Meet the women who drew upon their inner resilience and prevailed. Their vivid personal accounts provide inspiration to those who face daunting challenges, and offer a path forward. Each one of these brave, strong military spouses shares her personal tale of reuniting, recovering, and rebuilding with her catastrophically wounded warrior.

Wounded Warrior, Wounded Wife offers an intimate look into the chaotic and demanding lives of military spouses as they adjust to living with injured combat veterans. These women are thrust into caretaker roles for service members who return home with amputated limbs, brain injuries, burns, and disabilities, with virtually no support or training. Post-traumatic stress tears their families apart, and they must wrestle with huge, imposing questions: Does he still love me? Must I sacrifice my career forever? How will this affect my kids, my sex life, my happiness?

Wounded Warrior, Wounded Wife reveals the innermost thoughts of women who faced these challenges and prevailed—to not just survive, but thrive.

ABOUT THE AUTHOR

Barbara McNally is the author of *Unbridled: A Memoir*, a member of San Diego Writers Ink, and an active blog contributor to the *Huffington Post*. A licensed physical therapist, she has helped people from all walks of life, including veterans, recover and regain their strength. This work also connected her with the spouses of wounded warriors, and hearing their stories inspired her to launch the Barbara McNally Foundation, which is dedicated to offering workshops, seminars and scholarships that enhance the lives of women. The foundation also cosponsors Support, Purpose and Appreciation (SPA) Days for the spouses of wounded warriors, offering caregivers a much-needed day of relaxation and self-care.

PREFACE

Through my work, both as a physical therapist and as founder of the Barbara McNally Foundation, I have had the privilege of spending time with the wives and caregivers of hundreds of wounded warriors. With little warning and almost no training, these women have learned to serve their families as full-time caregivers while their partners try to recover from broken bones, lost limbs, severe head injuries, and other unspeakable assaults on their bodies and beings.

Each woman has a compelling story about how her life has changed since her husband returned home and where that journey has taken her. Over the past eight years, I've heard those stories twice a year at SPA Day—named for Support, Purpose, and Appreciation—which I sponsor for wives and caregivers of wounded warriors. More than 300 women apply for SPA Day, but at this time I am only able to accommodate thirty attendees.

Everyone gets a spa treatment in the morning, then we gather for lunch by the pool. During this mini-retreat, women share and connect with others who are experiencing parallel struggles. This sharing helps all of them build their coping skills and find useful resources. Women come to the Hotel del Coronado in Southern California from all over the United States, from as far away as Hawaii and Florida, for a weekend of much-needed restoration and rejuvenation.

The women—who might not know one another before SPA Day—quickly form bonds that few can fathom. They've all had similar life-altering experiences dealing with catastrophic challenges, both physical and emotional, and these shared experiences unite them in a kind of instant sisterhood. Although some start the spa sessions feeling guarded and a bit anxious, their warm natures and supportive spirits emerge as they open up to one another. They talk openly about broken marriages, ruined sex lives, and suicide attempts. They share the memories of violent confrontations, hurtful accusations, and the cold, silent stares of lovers made unrecognizable by posttraumatic stress. They share horrific hospital stories, awkward wheelchair anecdotes, and memories of deflecting uncomfortable looks from strangers.

For many women, SPA Day is the first time they've been away from their husbands, and the first day they've had to themselves in months or even years. After taking care of their spouses for so long, they've forgotten what it's like to pamper themselves. Most women don't come to SPA Day expecting to talk openly about their struggles, but almost all of them do so when they find themselves surrounded by nurturing, caring women who truly understand their circumstances. They recognize each other, because they are reflections of one another. SPA Day is about so much more than manicures and massages. It's about healing. The women's willingness to share their stories transforms the day. Those who have been holding on to the notion that they can "be strong and do anything" suddenly let their masks slip. They share their concerns, their fears, and their worries about the future in the first safe space many of them have known since their vet's return.

Theirs are stories of triumph and joy as well as disappointment and heartbreak, stories that are too rarely told in the media or public forums. I became inspired to share them here because they need and deserve to be heard. By bringing these stories to light, I hope to make more people aware that the struggles veterans face become struggles for their wives and family members, too. These stories are a tribute to the women who perform the selfless acts of strength and devotion necessary to live through the damage and pain of a spouse's military service having been cut short by devastating injuries.

These caretakers are the silent strength behind our soldiers, the troops on our home soil. Where there's a wounded warrior, there's a wounded lover—there's no way around it—and this is a topic that should be part of our national conversation.

So the next time you encounter a family with a wounded warrior, look for the woman by his side, and you will find someone who can teach you more about life than you ever dreamed possible. Read their stories here and learn from these women. Some names and identifying circumstances have been changed to protect their privacy.

Through the Barbara McNally Foundation, proceeds from this book's sales will provide more comfort, community building, healing opportunities, and leadership workshops for these committed and overworked women. For more information about these efforts, please visit www.BarbaraMcNally.com.

BARBARA MCNALLY
Barbara McNally Foundation

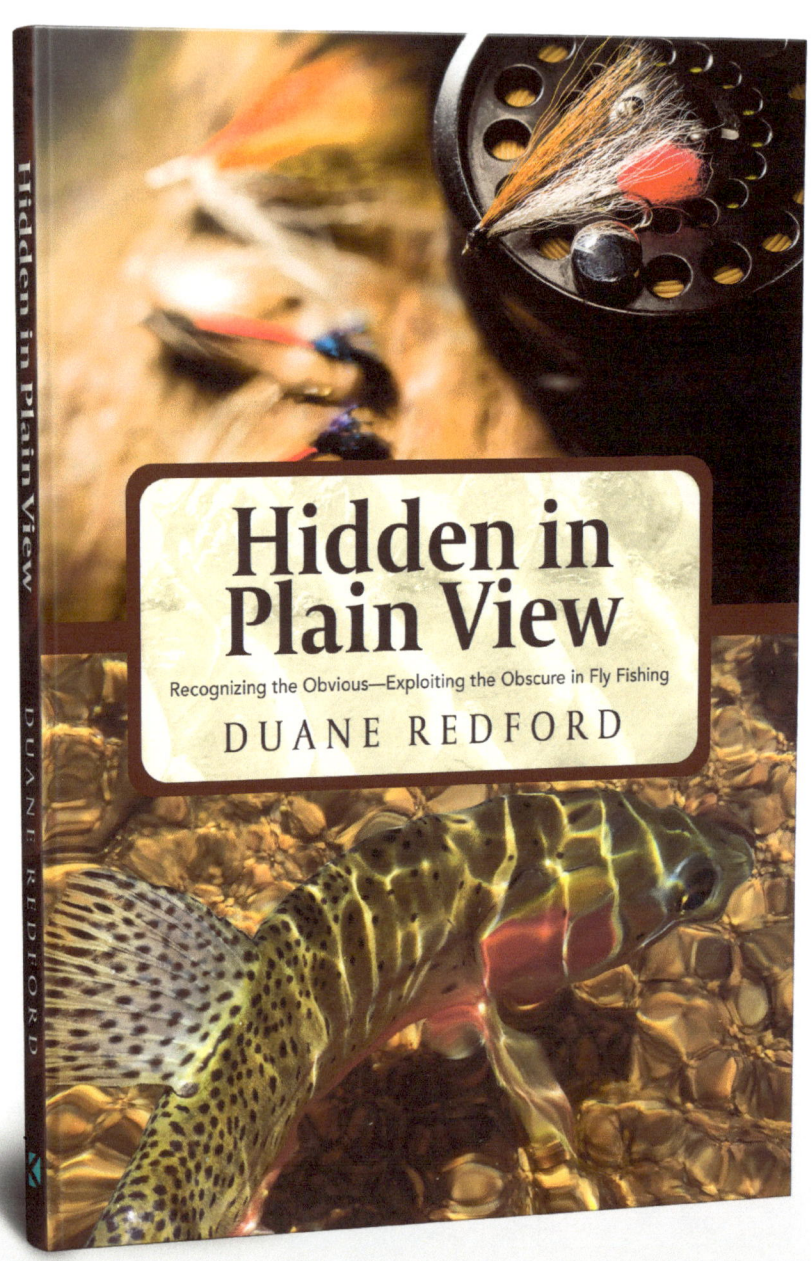

HIDDEN IN PLAIN VIEW

RECOGNIZING THE OBVIOUS— EXPLOITING THE OBSCURE IN FLY FISHING

by Duane Redford

PAGES: 222
PUB DATE: 12-10-2017
SOFTCOVER: $24.95, 978-1-63393-558-7
HARDCOVER: $36.95, 978-1-63393-560-0
EBOOK: $9.99, 978-1-63393-559-4

> "Whether you are a beginner or an expert, this book will help you take a huge step forward in your fly-fishing journey."
>
> —ROSS PURNELL, editor of *Fly Fisherman*

ABOUT THE BOOK

Ever wonder what the angler downstream of you catching fish in water you just fished is doing differently from you? Master angler and author Duane Redford delves into what the top 10 percent of anglers are seeing and doing differently from the fly fishing masses, and how they are consistently putting fish in the net in every situation. This work is a culmination of hundreds of hours on the river, observing and documenting insect, fish, and angler behaviors. It includes something for every level of angler from reading the obvious runs of the river to its subtle nuances, including bug selection made simple, how to rig to attain a lively drift, recognizing and exploiting the X-Y-Z grids in a river run, tactics to get better now, and how to implement the Fly Fishers' Formula while you locate and effectively fish your "quarter mile" of river. This book is a comfortable read that takes you with the author as he describes the techniques and applications derived from statistical information and observation, for successful fly fishing on any river, and it contains at least one "pearl on every page" to help any level angler get to the next mile marker on the journey to fly fishing wisdom. You are invited to catch more fish and find out what's *Hidden In Plain View*.

ABOUT THE AUTHOR

Duane Redford is a fly fishing guide from Colorado, a sought-after speaker, signature fly tyer for Montana Fly Company, Pro Staff lead for 8 Rivers Fly Rods, and author of *The Fly Fishers' Playbook, A Systematic Approach to Nymphing*, first and second editions. He can also be heard on Ask About Fly Fishing Internet Radio discussing fly fishing in an archived presentation. As a retired teacher and coach, Duane has a unique, observational and systematic approach to the river that he has used as the basis of his guiding and writing for dozens of years. This mental and physical approach, derived from guiding countless days on highly pressured, technical waters, has been refined over time, and is easily understood. When he's not guiding, Duane spends his time teaching fly fishing classes, tying flies, blogging, speaking across the country, and writing. When he's not teaching, writing or guiding, you'll find him on the river.

When it comes to fly fishing, if you're waiting on perfection, you're going to be waiting a long time. Fly fishing is like golf: you don't win it, you play it. You participate in hopes that you continually get better. Each time out becomes an opportunity to learn and improve. You can improve everything from casting to reading the water and the insect identification each time your boots get wet. The goal is to become proficient, better than proficient really, and the best way to accomplish this goal is to spend time on the river. Quality time.

I have been toting a fly rod for the better part of four decades. I've been blessed to fly fish many beautiful places. I feel as if I have always walked away from the river better than when I started. I want to improve every time out. As a former college baseball player, and high school baseball and football coach of many, many years, I tried to instill the same thoughts in my players. Be better today than you were yesterday. Find something to improve in your game through each experience, regardless if it's practice or a game. Each and every experience becomes a bona-fide learning experience, an opportunity to improve.

Experience has always been the best teacher; however, if you keep making the same mistakes, that mitigates the benefits. All you end up doing is reinforcing bad habits. I began playing baseball at the age of six, and continued through college. I remember going through hitting slumps from time to time. I would jump into the batting cage and hit until my hands bled. Unfortunately, in most cases, I was simply reinforcing bad habits that caused the slump in the first place. Furthermore, I was developing brand-new lousy habits at the same time. How in the world do you overcome that cycle?

After going through it countless times, it's my opinion that the best way to overcome a slump is by going back to the basics, recognizing the obvious, and exploiting the obscure. Sometimes this takes a qualified eye watching what you are doing from a distance; sometimes you can pull yourself out of the abyss. Either way, it takes a conscious effort.

If you're new to the sport of fly fishing and you are not catching fish, you're probably not capturing the basics of the sport. It might be your drift, it might be failure to recognize a fish eating your offering, or maybe you're not drifting the correct offerings at the correct speed and depths. There are certainly other factors that may be hindering your success, but typically, beginners suffer from those basic maladies.

How do you get out of that slump? Read everything you can, watch others do it properly, find a qualified eye to observe you, and fish, fish, fish. In other words, learn to recognize the obvious.

The obvious is what experienced fly fishers already know and take for granted. They are further down the road on the way to perfection. They see and adjust for conditions that are readily obvious for their skill level. They just know. The sooner you learn to recognize the obvious and "just know," the sooner you can advance to the next level, which includes the ability to exploit the obscure. More on the obscurities in fly fishing later.

The next level I will refer to is that of the intermediate angler. This angler knows the basic fundamentals of the cast, the drift, and "fish take" recognition, but aren't at the stage where they can recognize the obscurities of the sport. There are still holes in their game, but they can move fish. Most often, they don't know what they don't know, but their limited success keeps them hungry and coming back for more.

How does an intermediate angler battle a slump? By going back to the basics. Unlike the beginner, an intermediate has basic fundamentals to fall back on. These fundamentals may be less than desired or not perfectly aligned for quick progress, but the angler has enough skill to catch fish on their own. If a beginner is struggling with a nymph rig roll cast, a demonstration may be in order, but an intermediate angler only needs to be reminded of rod tip placement and paying attention to the rod tip path to get out of their roll-casting slump.

Let's take a look at what makes advanced anglers advanced. These guys and gals have all the fundamentals, characteristics, and mechanics figured out. They may still be mastering a specific skill, but these folks can flat-out fish. It takes a long time to get to this level and there is always more to learn or perfect, but that's the nature of the fly fishing beast. It's a game we play.

How does an advanced angler battle a slump? Generally, they battle slumps by exploiting the obscure. They have seen many things, and battled many conditions on many bodies of water. The experience level of some of these folks is legendary. I remember asking an old-timer once from across the river what he caught his last fish on. He looked at me wryly and shouted over the sound of the water, "Experience!" Not sure who got the bigger kick out of his reply, him or me.

Advanced anglers know how to fool fish, how to stay ahead of the hatch, and how to get a deeper understanding of fly fishing success. Let's say an advanced angler is nymphing a run, and is not hooking as many fish as usual. To him it's a slump, although most people would be satisfied with number of hook-ups. Capitalizing on what the river is giving obviously is easy, but there is something missing for this angler and he knows it. To overcome this slump, the advanced angler draws on knowledge and experience, and begins to examine where within the nymph drift he is getting hook-ups. This obscure tidbit will give him enough information to make many mini-adjustments to his rig, to exploit what most don't even recognize.

This book is designed to help the beginner to recognize what long-timers call the obvious, intermediates to begin the ascent into advanced level, and advanced anglers to take that last step into looking at the river differently than before.

I have stood with clients on the bridge off Highway 6 in Wolcott, Colorado, and watched men from many countries fish the Eagle River for the World Championships. The World Fly Fishing Championships pit elite competitors from twenty-seven countries against one another in a seven-day fly fishing event. These folks are the best of the best when it comes to catching fish on the fly. I always tell my clients to just observe and then tell me what they see. Every time I have had a client say something along the lines of "I would have never thought to fish that piece of water; how in the heck did he know there was a fish in there?"

I usually reply, "Yep, they are fishing where others won't because most don't recognize it as feeding water. That guy is simply exploiting the obscure."

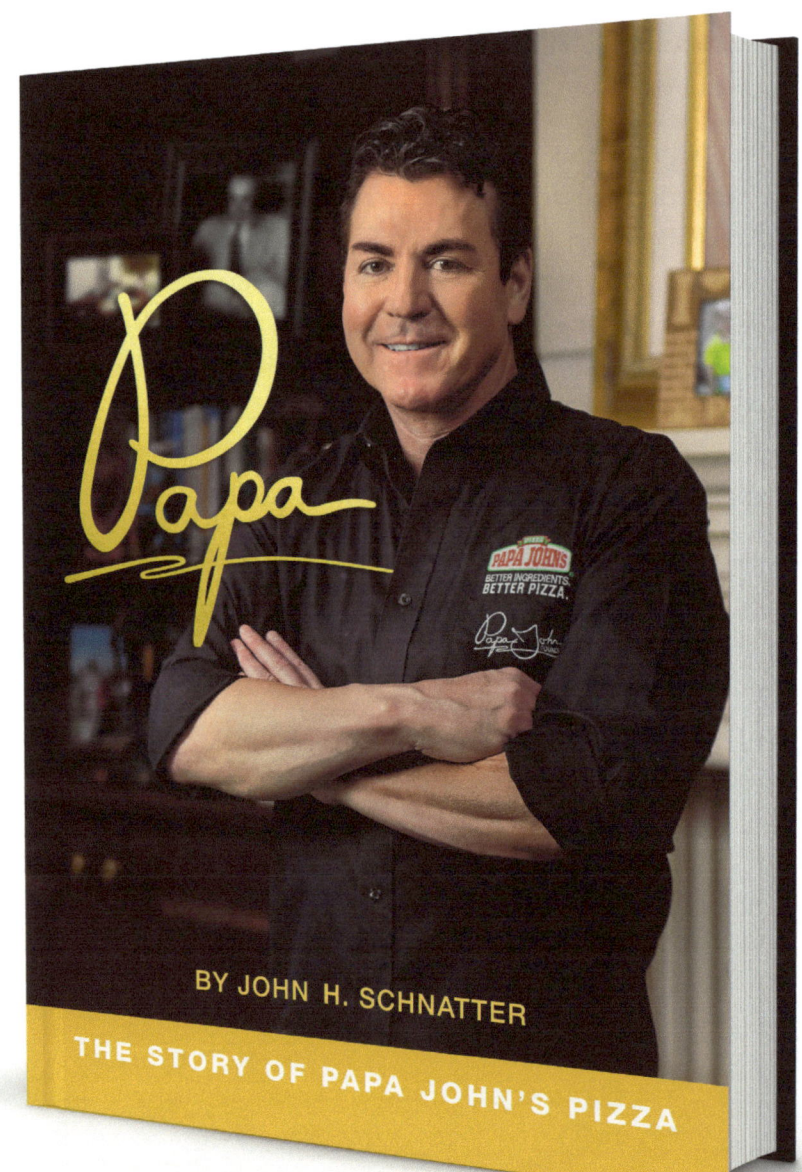

PAPA
THE STORY OF PAPA JOHN'S PIZZA

by John H. Schnatter

PAGES: 327

PUB DATE: 01-31-2017

HARDCOVER: $28.95 978-1-63393-386-6

EBOOK: $9.99 978-1-63393-385-9

ABOUT THE BOOK

Papa is the story of the American Dream. It's the story of starting small and making it big. It's a story that can inspire anyone to follow their passion and chart their own path. Whether you're looking for the principles and practices that make a business successful, or you're just looking to read the story of someone who achieved more than they ever thought possible, this book is for you. How does a pizza business go from a broom closet in the back of a rundown bar to a multinational chain with 5,000 stores and $3.7 billion per year in system-wide sales—and in only thirty years? The answer is simple: It puts its customers and its team members first. That's the story of Papa John's. That's the story of a "good business." And it could be the story of anyone who wants to run a company or benefit their community, so long as they're willing to apply the principles and practices that made Papa John's so wildly successful.

ABOUT THE AUTHOR

John H. "Papa John" Schnatter developed an entrepreneurial spirit and a passion for making pizzas while growing up in Jeffersonville, Indiana. So, after saving his father's bankrupt tavern at the age of twenty-two, he knocked down a broom closet in the back of the bar. Then he installed a used oven and began delivering pizza pies made with his personal recipe around town. Just over thirty years later, Papa John's is an international restaurant powerhouse. More importantly, John Schnatter insists on always using better ingredients to make better pizzas—pizzas that millions of people worldwide know and love.

Before Papa John's was ever a reality, it was an idea.

The idea was that we could use better ingredients to make a better pizza. This realization came to me as a fifteen-year-old washing dishes in the back of a local pizzeria. Seven years later, this idea inspired me to knock down a wall in a broom closet in the back of my father's bar so that I could start making my own traditional, superior-quality pizzas.

The idea worked well enough that I built a stand-alone pizzeria only a year later. Then I built a second, a tenth, a hundredth, a thousandth, and kept going. Papa John's hasn't stopped since. It never will.

My story is one of the American Dream. I didn't know what to expect when I made my first Papa John's pizza in that broom closet thirty-two years ago. But I did know that a principled business built on a solid foundation could achieve great things and improve people's lives. I believed we could create a popular pizzeria that kept my family well-taken care of, my team members well-paid and my community well-fed. I believed we could build a win-win-win relationship that left everyone better off. My goal was always to make a real and lasting difference in my hometown of Jeffersonville, Indiana. What I didn't realize was that a principled business could do so much more—that it could make the world a better place for millions of people far beyond my hometown.

That's what we've done over the past three decades. Today, Papa John's International, Inc. is one of the largest pizza companies in the world. As of this October, we operated 5,000 stores in forty countries and territories, with nearly 100,000 team members at franchise stores and 21,000 at corporate stores and had global system-wide sales of $3.7 billion, with 260 million pizzas sold every year. Every day, 600,000 people walk through the doors of a Papa John's store or open their front door to find a Papa John's pizza waiting for them.

But these numbers are only a reflection of what truly makes a difference in the world around us. Papa John's has succeeded because we make something that people want—something that benefits our team members, our customers, our shareholders, our suppliers, our franchisees and many more. Through innovation, respect for others and personal sacrifice, we have created a company that has brought people together and benefited millions throughout the world.

That is what truly matters. The proper role of business is to create jobs, grow wages and give people opportunities they otherwise would not have had.

Any business can do this, big or small. I have a particular fondness for small businesses—Papa John's started in a broom closet, after all. I believe the little guy is at the heart of our entire economic system. Some small businesses turn into larger businesses because they bring tremendous value into people's lives. Even the ones that stay small continue to provide jobs and joy in their local communities. No matter what form they take, entrepreneurship and innovation are the catalyst of human progress. And anyone—no matter who they are or where they came from—can contribute to this process if they're willing to try.

Ultimately, progress is what every entrepreneur should aspire to achieve—indeed, I believe every entrepreneur can achieve it, no matter what industry they're in or what product or service they sell. Human ingenuity and innovation are boundless. Anyone, regardless of their socioeconomic status or station in life, has the potential to find a new way to make the world a better place. It doesn't matter where they start or how small their first experiment is. It does matter that they remember that they can only help themselves by first helping others.

Fortunately, some business leaders are already engaged in this noble mission, which I call "good business." Yet many others—in fact, I believe that most others—are not. Instead, they engage in "bad business." By this I mean the type of business where they put their own self-interest above society's interests. They focus on short-term profits while neglecting long-term investments. They forgo quality in favor of mediocrity. They get bogged down by size or by bureaucracy or by falling into old habits that are hard to change. They "go to sleep," as I call it, and find it easier to break the rules or use unethical business practices. They take advantage of their people and treat them as objects of self-gain. They seek to handicap their competitors by using government to tilt the playing field in their own favor, using nefarious and devious business practices to benefit themselves at others' expense.

You need only look at the latest headlines to see just how rampant these problems are.

That's why I wrote this book. I hope to remind my fellow entrepreneurs of our real calling: to make the world around us a better place. That comes from my heart. I've seen firsthand how to do this—through innovation, respect for people and focus on quality. Just as Papa John's motto is "Better Ingredients, Better Pizza," so I believe that every company, big or small, should have the unofficial motto of "Better Business, Better World." It doesn't matter what words they use, so long as business leaders understand that their highest calling is to help themselves by first helping others.

I hope this book will help people understand how to do that. I have learned many lessons over the past four decades. I'm still learning lessons on a daily basis, and I don't expect that will ever change. There are always new and better ways to run a good business that makes other people's lives better.

For my part, I'm focused on finding out how to continue improving the quality of our traditional, superior-quality Papa John's pizzas.

Even more importantly, I want to continue helping Papa John's team members achieve their own personal potential. They truly put dignity into their labor. I hope to continue finding ways to reward them and help them find fulfillment in their lives. At the end of the day, Papa John's is in the people business more than it is in the pizza business. I have many examples of what works and how to think about situations and problems that businesses often confront. I have just as many examples—and probably more—of what doesn't work and how not to think. Over the course of this book, I'll introduce you to many of the concepts I've developed and adopted over the years. I hope that every chapter is filled with nuggets that will make you laugh, make you think and make you wonder how you can apply them—or improve them—in your own life.

YOUR BRIDAL STYLE

EVERYTHING YOU NEED TO KNOW TO DESIGN THE WEDDING OF YOUR DREAMS

by Rani St. Pucchi

PAGES: 350

PUB DATE: 12-20-2017

SOFTCOVER: $34.95 978-0-9976977-7-3

HARDCOVER: $45.95 978-0-9976977-9-7

EBOOK: $9.99 978-0-9976977-8-0

> "Rani St. Pucchi's designs are absolutely beautiful!"
>
> —ALISON KRAUSS, singer-songwriter

ABOUT THE BOOK

Your wedding day is possibly the most important day of your life, and your wedding dress may be the most important garment you will ever wear. Why not take control of the entire process of planning your ideal wedding—one that is fun, intimate and uniquely your own?

In Your Bridal Style, award-winning bridal designer Rani St. Pucchi shares her expert advice on everything a bride needs to create a truly unforgettable day, including:

- How to define your personal style based on your specific body type.
- Different wedding silhouettes and what is suitable for different venues and ceremonies.
- A helpful timeline for planning your wedding.
- Dos and don'ts for wedding dress shopping.
- Tips on choosing fabrics, colors, accessories and other finishing touches.
- How to avoid common wedding day mishaps.
- A FAQs section which answers 53 of your most pressing questions.
- Strategies for the photo shoot, and so much more.

This engaging, beautifully illustrated book is a treasure trove of ideas and inspiration. With this book in hand, any bride-to-be can design and create the wedding of her dreams.

ABOUT THE AUTHOR

Rani St. Pucchi, a trendsetting fashion designer whose expertise has been recognized in such media outlets as *Entertainment Tonight*, *Harper's Bazaar*, *Town and Country*, *Bride's*, *Cosmopolitan Bride*, *Martha Stewart Weddings* and *The Knot*, works to help women define the style that flatters them most—no matter what their age or stage of life, or what their body type is.

Introduction

There's something so powerful about going back in time and reliving the key moments of your life. Memories about events you had not thought about in a long time: what you have been through and where you have come from—a history of your successes, if you will.

And it begins with a dream . . .

For me, it all started with the hit television soap opera *Dallas*.

Friday nights were my favorite. I was hooked on the show, and in such awe of the glamorous clothes and the big hair the women wore, their lifestyle, the tall glass buildings—just about everything that *Dallas* stood for, and I visualized moving there one day.

I was living in Bangkok, Thailand, at the time running a tailoring business at a prestigious hotel. Although I had no design experience, I became quite proficient in designing women's ready-to-wear just because of my intense love of fashion and all things beautiful.

Dallas was my inspiration. I studied the extravagant fashion shown on the screen and would sketch for hours. It helped that I grew up around fine fabrics and laces, my family being the largest purveyors of fine lace in Thailand. Aside from my love of books, I had always lived and breathed fashion.

Among the affluent clientele I catered to in my tailoring salon was a beautiful lady from San Antonio, who visited me often. I would help her with her wardrobe and design her extravagant evening wear and suits. During one of her visits in 1984, she asked if I would support her charity event with my designs.

I couldn't believe it. Wasn't San Antonio close to Dallas?

I was excited beyond words, and before I knew it, I was on a flight to San Antonio with my fifty-two-piece ready-to-wear collection.

As I was preparing the collection and planning the order in which each outfit would appear, I thought it would be wonderful to have a wedding dress as the finale of the show. So, I whipped up a blush-colored Thai silk, hand-embroidered dress, and hand-beaded it with Swarovski crystals.

Little did I know that the one dress that I had designed as an afterthought would forever change my life. The show was a huge success, but more importantly, the roar that sounded when the finale dress came out on the runway was deafening!

The Universe works in mysterious ways. As luck would have it, the leasing agent of the Dallas Apparel Mart happened to be in the audience and invited me to bring my bridal collection to showcase at the Mart's Bridal Fashion Week that was happening in six months.

Wait! Should I not mention that my bridal collection consisted of just this ONE dress?

The ONLY bridal dress I had ever designed in my life . . .

But of course, *she* didn't need to know that. And I wasn't about to tell her!

For someone who had no design background and was clueless about wedding dresses, it was a daunting thought.

My heart was beating so fast . . .

Dallas! This was a dream come true.

I hesitated, wondering if I had the talent, and more importantly, the money and the resources to honor such a huge commitment. But that thought only lasted a split second as I found myself saying, "Yes, of course! I would be honored."

As someone who had spent years dreaming about one day living in Dallas, I was totally convinced that the opportunity given me was nothing less than a divine intervention. I had a fire in my heart and a calling on my life that I trusted would play out.

I had more questions than answers right then. When I had the dream of one day living in Dallas, I had no clue as to what career I would follow, nor how I would be led there. All I knew was that perhaps, if I stopped mulling and stressing over the "how" and just followed that small tug on my heart, then it would lead me right where I needed to be.

And so here I was. Saying "yes" to my dream.

THINKING OUTSIDE THE BOTTLE

THE PRODUCT ENTREPRENEUR'S PLAYBOOK

by Duane Thompson
with Cheryl Ross

PAGES: 234

PUB DATE: 7-15-2017

SOFTCOVER: $19.95 978-0-99701-630-7

HARDCOVER: $29.95 978-1-63393-355-2

EBOOK: $9.99 978-0-99701-631-4

SELF PUBLISHED BY DUANE THOMPSON

ABOUT THE BOOK

In *Think Outside the Bottle: The Product Entrepreneur's Playbook*, self-made multimillionaire Duane Thompson draws product entrepreneurs a blueprint for business success. This fast-paced, engaging how-to guide shows how he built his business up from a pot of salsa he created in his college dorm room to a seven-figure-grossing company with products sold on the East Coast and beyond—and how you can take your product from concept to reality too. The *Playbook* pushes and prods you to brainstorm ideas that will help you create the best product possible. It provides plenty of practical advice on how to develop your brand, select the right manufacturer, and get free media coverage. It also takes you through fourteen steps to develop your product—and that's just for starters. If you're serious about taking your business dream to the next level of success, the *Playbook* is for you!

ABOUT THE AUTHOR

Duane Thompson is the founder, president, and CEO of Sabrosa Foods Inc., a Hampton Roads, Virginia-based food-manufacturing and service company selling products in the United States and abroad. Duane and his company's award-winning salsa, Asorbas, have been featured in print, online, and on TV, including MSNBC and CNBC. *Inside Business*, the Hampton Roads business journal, named Duane 2010 Entrepreneur of the Year and a Top 40 Under 40 businessperson. Duane lives in Norfolk, Virginia, with his wife, Lingisi, and son, Duane Jr.

PREFACE

YEARS AGO, WHEN I was first trying to make my way as a product entrepreneur, a rep at the local Small Business Development Center looked at me like I had six arms when I revealed I was selling a product— one that I was growing, manufacturing, and distributing locally—not a service. She was surprised to learn I was selling a special-recipe blend I'd perfected in my own kitchen—and she wasn't the only one. Others, including friends, wanted to know why I was investing so much time trying to launch a salsa when I already had a very well-paying job. Given the dramatic decrease in product manufacturing in the United States over the last several decades and our culture's emphasis on working for others, it's no wonder people were perplexed. To answer their question, I told them I make and sell salsa for a personal reason and because I strongly believe the US needs more product entrepreneurs who create and sell their own goods. I want to help this country reinvigorate product manufacturing. It's about building a stronger US dollar and making the US sustainable. As the old saying goes, "It starts with me." So I've written Think Outside the Bottle: The Product Entrepreneur's Playbook to help Americans who have created a product, dream to create a product, or have a product in the works. I want to see more of us introduce new products into the marketplace—products created, produced, manufactured, and sold in the States. Think Outside the Bottle can help you find success while also helping our country. A little history: In the course of running my own product business, I've tried to understand the scope of US product manufacturing by researching its decline over past decades, and as result, its impact on the US economy. The info I gleaned jarred me. I cannot get some of the stats out of my mind. Bureau of Labor Statistics show just how damaging product manufacturing losses have been to the US. Between 1970 and 2009, US goods–producing jobs shrank from 39 percent of the private–sector workforce to 17 percent. Meanwhile, we've had to borrow more to pay for things made elsewhere, and wouldn't you know it, middle– class workers have suffered the most. Service-sector jobs that replaced manufacturing jobs paid an average weekly wage of $610, compared with $810 in the goods-producing sector. Between 2000 and 2009 alone, median household incomes dropped 4 percent because of the disappearance of solid manufacturing jobs. If you didn't see why a push to increase product manufacturing in the US was important before, I hope these startling stats help you now understand. To become a financially stronger country, the US needs to get back to creating and manufacturing more of its own goods. But still, while you may want to create a product, and you may agree with me that this would boost US manufacturing and innovation, maybe you're not convinced that manufacturing your own product in America is a good business move for you (there is a difference between creating and manufacturing, which you'll learn about as you get deeper into this book). You may be thinking, Why should I choose a US manufacturer when there could be less expensive options overseas? First, depending on the type of product you're making, working with overseas manufacturers won't necessarily be less expensive. And that's just for starters. Shipping products from overseas can be very expensive, and once a product reaches the States, it still has to be shipped around the country to customers, which means you're paying foreign and domestic shipping costs. Another consideration is speed of delivery. Weather or unexpected travel accidents can delay overseas shipments, which means postponed sales; or your products could get damaged during long periods of travel. Durable goods, like food products, are especially vulnerable. Another demerit: It is harder to supervise overseas production— that's if you're able to supervise production at all. You'll either have to frequently visit the manufacturing site or send someone from your company (either for frequent visits or to live) to oversee every step of the process. Consider that there may be a language barrier between you and your manufacturer too. If you or your traveling employee don't know the manufacturer's language, you have to hope and trust that at least one of the manufacturer's staffers—for your sake, one who knows enough about your product to watch over the manufacturing process—speaks fluent English. Some of the benefits of manufacturing in the States should now be obvious—communication issues between you and your manufacturer should be minimal, if any; by doing business domestically, and especially if your manufacturer is in the same area as your business, you can transport your products to your customers at the lowest price in the shortest time, which can mean higher sales and profits and fewer logistical headaches. And if you care about the impact of your business decisions on our country's economy as well as your business's bottom line, then this should make you smile: Manufacturing in the States can create more jobs here and a better environment for selling your product. More people with jobs is more people who have the resources to buy your goods. The importance of being an American product entrepreneur can't be overstated. In this role, you have the potential to fortify our economy with jobs and paychecks. You can create an economic ripple that lifts all ships. Now that we've put this topic in its proper place, let's get down to brass tacks. Let's lift the economy by helping you become a successful product entrepreneur.

Duane Thompson

President and CEO, Sabrosa Foods Inc.
Norfolk, VA
www.sabrosafoods.com

UNITED WAY WOMEN OF PHILANTHROPY: 100 WOMEN UNITED

PAGES: 32

PUB DATE: 10-15-2015

ABOUT THE BOOK

At 900 strong, the Women's Leadership Council works toward improving the lives of women and children in need throughout South Hampton Roads. Through leadership, fundraising and advocacy, we pool resources, solve problems, and lend our muscle to projects all across the community.

One Woman Can Make a Difference

One Hundred Can Remake a Community

ORGANIZATIONS YOUR CONTRIBUTIONS FUNDED

Career Start—Certified Nursing Assistant training

Catholic Charities—anger management program

Dwelling Place—parenting skills to prevent family violence & post-shelter support

ForKids—GED preparation for mothers

Genieve Shelter—job preparation for victims of domestic violence

Girls on the Run—race training to build emotional, social & physical health

Girl Scouts, Colonial Coast—at P.B. Young, Sr. & Tidewater Park elementary schools

Girl Scouts, Virginia Beach Juvenile Detention Center—a full education/social program

Hampton Roads Youth Center—teaching girls self-esteem & independence

HER Shelter- Sweet Haven Bakery—job training for women fleeing domestic violence

Old Dominion University CARE Now—a character building & enrichment program

P.B. Young, Sr. Elementary School—incentivized field trips, Raising A Reader program

Planning Council—day care support for low-income families

Reach, Inc.—literacy program for shelter families

Salvation Army—transitioning single mothers & children from homelessness

Samaritan House—rapid re-housing/housing for homeless or abused women

Seton House—mentoring children of prisoners

The Up Center Parents as Teachers—helping parents become their child's first teacher

Virginia Social Ventures Spotlight Books—job training & placement

Virginia Beach Community Development Corp.—up to 2 years housing for the homeless

YWCA of South Hampton Roads—quality, affordable child care for parents attending TCC

THE 10 for 10 STORY
STRENGTH IN NUMBERS

Founding and growing the *10 for 10* into what we call the Women of Philanthropy has been very much like a relay: each racer handing the baton to another who runs with the idea and expands the scope. In 2004 Paige Romig, the Women's Leadership Council's first chair person, campaigned to create an endowment. Marianne Dickerson endowed the initial gift of $85,000, and Paige was the first to include the Women's Leadership Council Endowment Fund (WLCEF) in her estate planning.

As next chair in 2005, Marianne championed the WLCEF endowment effort by recruiting Jane Batten, Joan Brock and Susan Goode to provide a $100,000 challenge match. When donors stepped up to this challenge, the core group was so encouraged that they conceived the *10 for 10* theme and launched an ongoing campaign.

By 2006, with Marianne leading the charge and UWSHR's Michele Anderson coaching, they had convinced 10 women to each pledge $10,000. Soon another 10 entered the equation—making this a ten-year effort to ultimately raise $1 million.

A number of women were instrumental in bringing this to fruition, but none more so than Joan Brock. Throughout, Joan has kept the momentum going—organizing, recruiting and inspiring everyone to think big. In turn, Joan is inspired by her belief in the difference we can make as a united force, an impact beyond anything we might accomplish individually.

As word of the *10 for 10* grew, recruitment became easier. By our tenth year, several women stepped up to be members without waiting to be asked. We are now 100 strong with an endowment of $2.5 million. And that number includes working women, new moms and others who have sacrificed to make the pledge. Through the power of our collaborative efforts, we've grown from a fundraising initiative to become a voice for women's philanthropy and a model for other communities. We are empowered women empowering women, 10 by 10 for 10 years. In that alone, this is very much a story about the incalculable strength that lies in numbers.

— Women of Philanthropy Steering Committee

(LEFT TO RIGHT) MARIANNE DICKERSON, JOAN BROCK & PAIGE ROMIG

HEALTH

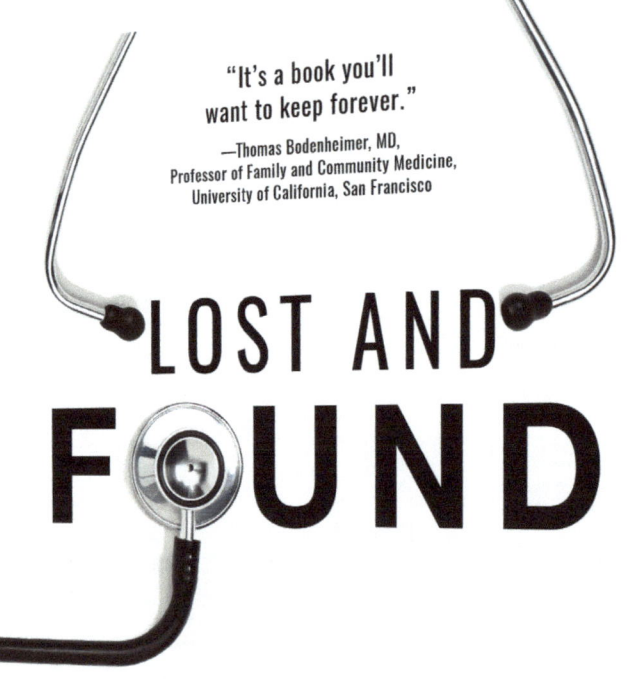

LOST AND FOUND

A CONSUMER'S GUIDE TO HEALTHCARE

by Peter B. Anderson, MD
and Paul H. Grundy, MD

with Tom Emswiller and Bud Ramey

PAGES: 248

PUB DATE: 11-15-2015

SOFTCOVER: $16.95 978-1-63393-186-2

HARDCOVER: $24.95 978-1-63393-188-6

EBOOK: $7.99 978-1-63393-187-9

> "It's a book you'll want to keep forever."
>
> —THOMAS BODENHEIMER, MD, professor of Family and Community Medicine, University of California, San Francisco

ABOUT THE BOOK

Regardless of your politics, personal opinions, or individual experience, it's difficult to deny that the American healthcare system is broken and in desperate need of repair. These and related questions about healthcare are being asked all across the country:

Why can't my doctor be more accessible and accommodating when I need an appointment?

What is the "right" medical care and how would I know it when I experience it?

How can I get personalized and reliable information to help make decisions about my family's health?

Why is healthcare so expensive and can I ever expect it to be more affordable?

How do I choose the right insurance plan for my family?

What programs or assistance are available when I just don't have the money to see a doctor or pay for medications?

What does the future of healthcare look like and will it be better than the present?If you're wondering about the same and similar kinds of issues, *Lost and Found* will be a resource you'll want to keep close at hand and turn to again and again.

ABOUT THE AUTHOR

Paul Grundy, MD, MPH, FACOEM, FACPM, currently serves as IBM's global director of healthcare transformation and is a member of the IBM Industry Academy. He attended medical school at the University of California, San Francisco, completed his residency training in preventive medicine and a postdoctoral fellowship in occupational health in the international environment, both at Johns Hopkins. Dr. Grundy also earned a master's degree in public health at the University of California, Berkeley. He is a member of the National Academy of Science's Institute of Medicine, Chair of Health Policy for the Employee Retirement Income Security Act (ERISA) and an adjunct professor at the University of Utah Department of Family and Preventive Medicine. In 2014, Dr. Grundy was named as ambassador for Healthcare DENMARK, a role in which he shares best practices from the Danish healthcare system with U.S. and international physicians. Prior to his career at IBM, Dr. Grundy was a medical officer and flight surgeon in the US Air Force and served in the US Department of State, where he advised ambassadors on healthcare programs for diplomatic posts. He received the Department of State Superior Honor Award for efforts related to the HIV/AIDS crisis in sub-Saharan Africa. Dr. Grundy also served as chief medical officer for the Adventist Health System, Pennsylvania, and is currently president of the Patient-Centered Care Collaborative, a not-for-profit advocacy group committed to advancing an effective health system built on a strong foundation of primary care and the patient-centered medical home. Dr. Grundy is widely known as "the godfather of the medical home." You can follow Dr. Grundy on Twitter at @Paul_PCPCC. Dr. Paul Grundy may be the most knowledgeable person in the United States regarding the state of our country's healthcare." —Craig Jones, M.D., Executive Director, Vermont Blueprint for Health

health reform, Dr. Anderson is also a frequent national speaker and media contributor on family practice and primary care issues. To learn more about Dr. Anderson and his work, visit teamcaremedicine.com or follow @thefamiliarphys on Twitter. "I spent several days with Dr. Anderson and his team to see this innovative practice style firsthand. I quickly became convinced that this was how primary care, and primary care physicians, could survive . . ." —Kevin Hopkins, M.D. Cleveland Clinic Family Practice Management

Dr. Anderson completed his MD at the University of Virginia School of Medicine and his residency training at Riverside Regional Medical Center in Newport News, Virginia. He maintained a large primary care practice for thirty years, which became the first in the state of Virginia to be recognized and accredited by the National Committee for Quality Assurance (NCQA) as a medical home. While in practice, Dr. Anderson also served as clinical assistant professor of family medicine at the University of Virginia School of Medicine and assistant professor of Clinical Family and Community Medicine at Eastern Virginia Medical School. After retiring from active practice, he founded and now leads Team Care Medicine™, a healthcare consulting and training company. Using a model of inside-the-exam-room care that serves to both redesign traditional workflow patterns and elevate staff responsibilities, Dr. Anderson has helped over 300 physician practices, as well as US Department of Defense Military Health primary care clinics, transform their practices. The author of three books, including *The Familiar Physician*, which focuses on the patient-physician bond and the patient-centered medical home as key elements of primary care medicine and

FOREWORD:

We have a love-hate relationship with our American healthcare system, and the "love" part is no mystery. We enjoy the world's most technologically advanced resources, sophisticated interventions, and highly trained medical specialists. Our level of emergency and trauma care is unequaled. When it comes to accommodating people with disabilities, carrying out research, or developing drugs for rare diseases, it doesn't get any better.

So what's not to love? Well, to begin with, the costs are overwhelming. Paying more for our care than anyone else in the world might seem like a fair tradeoff except for the inconvenient fact that our life expectancy is lower than virtually all other developed nations. This crushing expense may be inevitable in a technology-based health system that's fragmented and wasteful and set up to pay for volume rather than quality, and it threatens the financial security of growing numbers of individuals, families, and businesses.

When you add in the difficulty that millions of Americans experience trying to gain timely access to primary care, our high rate of chronic disease and a recent report in the *Mayo Clinic Proceedings* that indicates many long-accepted medical procedures aren't really doing much good, it's easy to understand the source of all the frustration and dissatisfaction.

The good news is that there are some beams of light shining through, and they're focused on our ability to move from passive acceptance of a broken healthcare system to active participation in making it better. Toward that objective, this book was created to help you improve the way you use and pay for healthcare, not only for the purpose of saving money, but also for being able to make informed choices for you and your loved ones that lead to better health.

The information that follows can help you navigate the obstacles that stand between you and high-quality, affordable healthcare. You'll read about why primary care, more than any other aspect of medicine, will determine the quality of our healthcare as a nation. Along the way you'll get a close-up view of one of the essential elements in healthcare reform, the Patient-Centered Medical Home. You'll see the value inherent in a strong patient-physician relationship and how a "familiar physician" delivers the best preventive and acute care and chronic care management. You'll learn how skilled healthcare teams, partnering with you as an essential member, can provide the right care at the right time in the right place. And you'll find out how to save money without sacrificing quality in today's changing healthcare environment.

Your guides on this journey of discovery are Dr. Peter Anderson and Dr. Paul Grundy, two physicians who bring a unique combination of personal experience and expertise to the quest for affordable and effective healthcare. Over the past decade, their tireless and innovative efforts on behalf of primary care medicine have received national recognition in both the medical and business communities. Their commitment to sharing that experience and restoring primary care to the foundation of American medicine is the basis of this book.

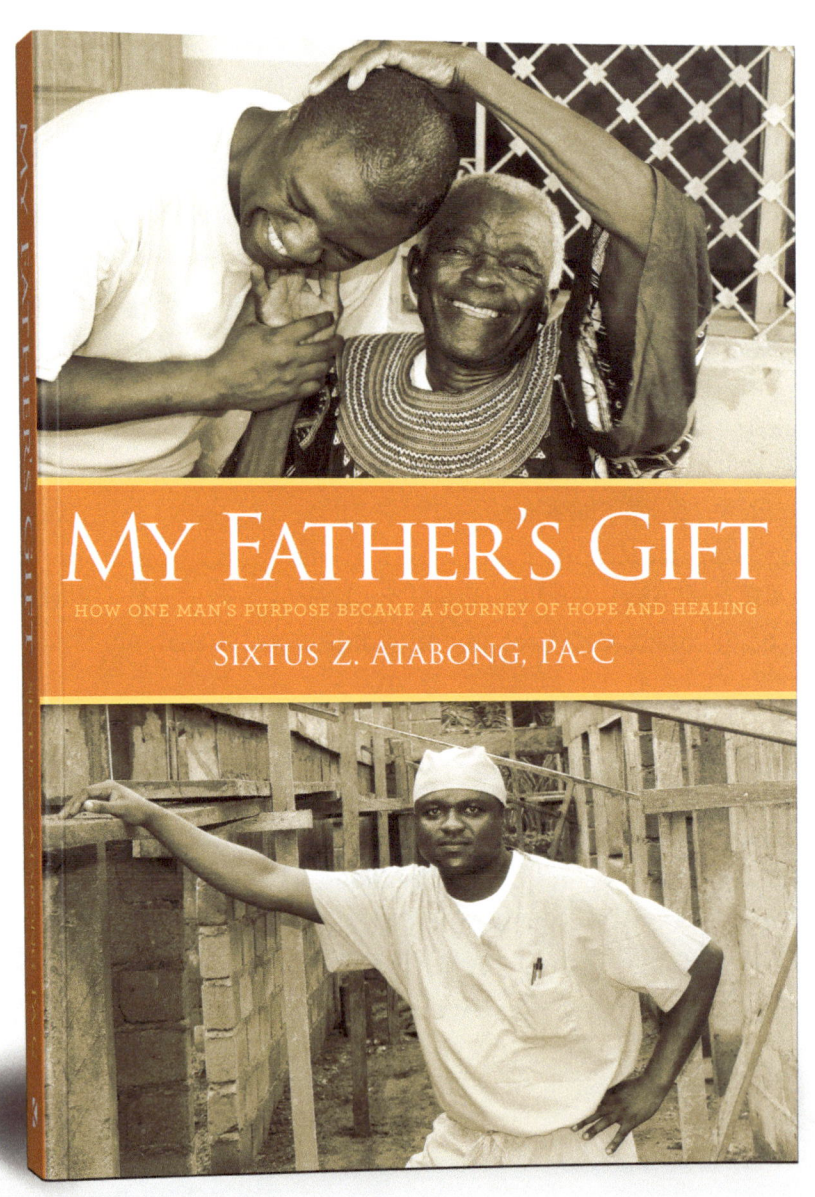

MY FATHER'S GIFT

HOW ONE MAN'S PURPOSE BECAME A JOURNEY OF HOPE AND HEALING

by Sixtus Z. Atabong, PA-C

PAGES: 316

PUB DATE: 8-24-2018

SOFTCOVER: $19.95, 978-1-63393-675-1

HARDCOVER: $26.95, 978-1-63393-676-8

EBOOK: $9.99, 978-1-63393-677-5

> "This book will inspire you to love more, live more and serve more. It is a must-read for all PAs!"
>
> —LINDA C. DELANEY, MPAS, PAC, past president of the Texas Academy of Physician Assistants, past director at large of the American Academy of Physician Assistants

ABOUT THE BOOK

Born into a poor West African family in the disease-stricken town of Fontem, John N. Atabong embarked into the unknown in search of hope. He was eleven, but he triumphed against all odds to give his children the best care and education available. Eventually, he sacrificed his most valuable possession, his son Sixtus, sending him to study in the United States with nothing more than lessons learned from his days working the farms and his father's basic biblical teachings. Sixtus Atabong's journey of temptations and challenges in the US gives rise to a mission: to give back. He uses his gift to extend God's healing hands and unfailing love to the far corners of the earth through sustainable health care infrastructures. Fulfilling his father's dream, Sixtus hopes that he too can leave the world a better place than he found it.

ABOUT THE AUTHOR

Sixtus Z. Atabong, PA-C, is a practicing neurosurgery physician assistant. He is also the president and founder of Purpose Medical Mission, a nonprofit organization that focuses on developing sustainable healthcare infrastructures and services in developing countries. He is a recipient of numerous local and national awards for his leadership and humanitarian work around the world. Sixtus and his wife, Kyu Mee, have two young boys and live in Lubbock, Texas.

INTRODUCTION

I was invited by a friend for an early Saturday morning coffee at Starbucks to meet with a gentleman from Austin, Texas who had done extensive mission work in East Africa. He is a successful businessman who was born in Snyder, a small town in West Texas. He was visiting his family to celebrate his grandfather's 90th birthday. They had helped build a church and provide solar energy to several communities in South Sudan. While in South Sudan, he was touched by the complete lack of healthcare in the region and was praying for guidance on how he could help. Not being in the medical field, he faced many challenges. His goal was to help the people build a sustainable medical clinic. He wanted to seek my advice.

We spent two hours talking about each other's work and the fulfillment that comes with saying "yes" to a call to serve. I was seeing him off to his car, and he asked me, his full cup of coffee still in his hand, how I ended up in West Texas. We both had a very busy day ahead, so I gave him a brief version of my own story. He then asked me if I had ever considered writing a book about my life. I thanked him and told him that I didn't write, but he persisted. If not a book, he said, I needed to keep a journal or write a memoir for my kids, as no one would be able to tell my story better. The last thing he said to me before getting in his car was, "Sixtus, you should aspire to inspire before you expire."

Well, David, thank you. Here we go . . .

As a child, I never understood why Dad proudly accepted the villagers' nickname *Idi Amin Dada*. It was a nickname he acquired after the infamous president of Uganda from 1971 to 1979, who was portrayed in the 2007 movie, *The Last King of Scotland,* as the eccentric brutal Ugandan dictator. To the young men in my village, the name might have been well deserved. For me, he was just Pa John Atabong—my father, my inspiration, my hero.

Pa John was born in Bellah Ngeh, into a polygamous family with three wives, during a period of extreme poverty and an infant mortality rate of over 90 percent. He came into this world in his parents' house, made of red mud, roofed with thatches, and located on one of the many steep hills of what is now commonly called Fontem, in the South West Region of Cameroon, West Africa. He was the last of his mother's twelve children, only three of whom would survive into adulthood. Nine of his siblings had died at birth or during their first few years of life, leaving my father and two older brothers. There is no document of his date of birth, so any reference to his age would be an estimate based on a timeline of stories gathered from him and family members.

His parents had a small farm where they raised crops, mostly for home consumption. Though my grandparents had no formal education, they wanted to send their children to school. They couldn't afford to send all three boys to school, and they still needed help on the farm. They decided to pick the most intelligent of the boys to send to primary school. After months of secretly observing the boys, they picked the second oldest son. My dad was devastated, but at the age of ten there was nothing he felt he could do about that decision. He still wanted to go to school like a few of his friends in the village.

Just a year after his brother started primary school, their father died, leaving behind his mother to care for them. Without a husband, she neither could afford her son's education or food for her family. She desperately needed to find a way to support her three young boys, so she met with a local witch doctor who was also a traditional healer and a fortune teller. The healer advised my grandmother to take her three sons out of the village to escape a jealous witch who was killing off rivals through witchcraft. During this time, the Bangwa people of Fontem mostly practiced traditional medicine with traditional healers as their doctors, and local chiefs were rulers. Witchcraft was widely accepted and practiced. This was a time when women were seen and considered as second-class citizens who couldn't own property and were not allowed to work outside the home. World War II was still being fought, and the fear was that developed nations were recruiting fighters from their foreign colonies. If my grandmother took her sons to the coast, they could be forced to fight in a foreign war or work in plantations with little or no compensation.

By the age of eleven, my father had become quite skilled at harvesting palm oil and selling the produce at the local village markets. The work was quite labor intensive, but he needed to support his family and help pay for his brother's education. His work involved climbing thirty-plus-feet-tall palm trees to harvest the palm nuts. Then he would spend days, with the help of his mother, producing the palm oil. Compared to the other villagers, he had become quite successful. But my grandmother, afraid he might get harmed by the local "witches" out of jealousy, sent her son to live with a family friend in a distant village called Letia. My father's newly adopted father was nicknamed Pa Moni.

AUTISM UNCENSORED

PULLING BACK THE CURTAIN

by Whitney Ellenby

PAGES: 338

PUB DATE: 03-15-2017

SOFTCOVER: $19.95 978-1-63393-413-9

HARDCOVER: $29.95 978-1-63393-415-3

EBOOK: $4.99 978-1-63393-253-1

> "... an unflinching exploration of a mother's emotional—and, at times, physical—struggle for the dignity and humanity of her autistic son. A brave book."
>
> —RON SUSKIND, author of *Life, Animated: A Story of Sidekicks, Heroes, and Autism*

ABOUT THE BOOK

"And when in the grips of a public tantrum, amidst the horror and humiliation of him shrieking and splayed out on the floor while strangers recoiled in shock, my mind lurched towards an inescapable truth—that I want out from this nightmare. I want out from this child."

So begins the turbulent ride of one parent's decision, crafted in despair and desperation, to abandon traditional interventions for her autistic son in favor of a "hands on" approach of repeatedly exposing her son to real-world settings. *Autism Uncensored* is an unrestricted portal into the mind of someone who had no intention of sacrificing her career or life for autism, unaware of the many ways it would irreversibly redefine both. As she clarifies at the outset, "this is not the story of a miraculous breakthrough or recovery." Zack is still very much autistic and always will be. It is instead the true, real-time account of her decision to allow Zack to indulge in the very behaviors that formal therapies sought to extinguish, to disclose Zack's diagnosis in public settings, and to repeatedly expose him to real-world situations and override his tantrums regardless of public ridicule or scorn.

Autism Uncensored goes where no other book dares—revealing the private disgrace and self-blame about having a "defective" child; the near disintegration of marriage; the failure of the traditional behavioral interventions; and the mercenary way in which service providers prey on parents' desperation for a cure. It is a personal manifesto about how a socially integrated life is attainable regardless of whether a child overcomes the major limitations of autism, sparking a new conversation which goes beyond simply accepting persons with autism for who they are, but considers pushing them beyond their comfort zones to learn who they are capable of becoming. An unstoppable ride with jolting twists and turns, *Autism Uncensored* will leave you exhilarated, informed and still gasping for air.

ABOUT THE AUTHOR

Whitney Ellenby is a former US Department of Justice disability rights attorney whose writings have been published in *The Washington Post*, a law review periodical, and the US DOJ website. She is the author of "Divinity vs. Discrimination: Curtailing the Divine Reach of Church Authority," Golden Gate University Law Review (1996)), as well as an amicus brief on behalf of the US DOJ Disability Rights Division regarding discrimination against mobility-impaired individuals in violation of the Americans with Disabilities Act (ADA). She is the proud parent of a son with Autism and founder of "Autism Ambassadors," a charitable venture through which she runs exclusive recreational events for over 600 families impacted by Autism in the Washington, DC/Maryland area, including a sensory-friendly showing of the world-famous "Gazillion Bubbles Show." She is an expert on Autism and has testified before the Maryland senate on disability-related issues, is a member of the Developmental Disabilities Advisory Council for Montgomery County, MD, and serves on the University of Maryland Autism Spectrum Disorder Advisory Board. Whitney's expertise is steeped in her extensive disability law background, personal experience with her own son, and over ten years of serving children, teens and adults with Autism of all ages through her "Autism Ambassador" events. Her monthly "Ambassador events" have been featured in local TV news, *The Washington Post*, *Bethesda Magazine*, and *The Bethesda Gazette*. Whitney was most recently honored with an Autism Awareness Proclamation and Community Leader award for her advocacy and dedication to the disability community of Maryland. She has what she describes as a "healthy obsession" with all things Autism.

"INTRO"

When I considered writing about the toll of autism I was determined to do so only if I had something new to say. To do so, I would have to be unflinchingly honest, providing unvarnished accounts of the brutality of autism both on the afflicted and those who love and care for them. Some experiences of the human condition are so serious and life-altering that only the unguarded truth can do them justice. People with autism, and those who care for them, are so precious and worthy that their lives must be lived without regard to the uninformed opinions or fears of others who have not walked in their shoes.

My story feels useful only if I reveal not just the unorthodox actions I chose to pursue with my son, but also the internal dialogue that provoked them. The portrait I paint involves dark thoughts and confessions some might find ugly, abhorrent or even excruciating, but an honest account of my journey demands that I reveal them. My goal in writing *Autism Uncensored* is to provide unguarded disclosures that might allow others in pain to know you are not alone, and that your situation can indeed improve.

Some experiences must be lived firsthand to be truly understood. My story is true and delivered in the first person, present tense, precisely to capture the reality I have lived. In telling my story I am talking directly to you, the reader, as if I am living the experience now—-and placing you inside my head. You will not be hovering in the remote corners of these pages observing from a detached perspective: as I'm cobbled on the floor, you will be down on the floor with me. I am reliving the seminal moments of my life and so, through my writing, have reset my mind back in time. I attempt to conjure the emotions roiling inside me, actual inner dialogue, and exact conversations in their genuine, excruciating detail. My intent is to provide a verbatim account—what I actually felt, heard, smelled, thought and said at the time. If my recounting is imperfect, it's still overwhelmingly accurate.

Please know as you read that I am not speaking *for* other parents with autistic children, but rather *to* them, as well as to anyone sensitive enough to take the extraordinary ride. Autism is not easy; to pretend otherwise would betray what I and so many others experience on a daily basis. Revealing my innermost thoughts—and risk being publicly judged for them—is the price I pay for speaking my truth.

A more serious cost of being wholly uncensored is the betrayal of my son, Zack, whose limited verbal skills make it impossible for me to have the type of dialogue with him that would allow him to consent to such an intimate telling of our story. I may never know the breadth of his private feelings about me and what happened between us, just as he may never fully know mine. I've wrestled mightily with issues of disclosure and betrayal across many subjects in this book, but in the end I came down on the side of disclosure because Zack—the most unpretentious and courageous person I've ever known—is a living embodiment of "real-world" progress in the often inscrutable world of autism. In my heart I believe that he would approve of giving others what he has given me: an education that cannot be taught through words alone but through direct exposure to live situations. It is the immediacy of our experience which I seek to reproduce, and my hope is to impart unexpected truths and discoveries about autism worthy of the trust you have placed in me by reading my words.

So I start with a singular truth—that to live with an autistic child is to experience great joy and exquisite pain in equal measure.

Zack is a stunning, angel-faced child with the purest of hearts. But from the moment he was diagnosed with autism at nineteen months old, my world quite literally changed forever. There was an immediate and jolting disconnect between me and other parents that continues to this day and will remain for the rest of my life. As a toddler, it was *my* child who spun senselessly in circles, made conspicuous yelping noises and screeched loudly whenever I dared to redirect him. I was the only mother to shadow my toddler in every gym and music class, desperately pinning his legs to the floor to get him to follow the routines without spiraling off into his own world. If my son was mixed in with a group of children and there were sudden piercing shrieks, I knew without looking it was him, making me feel as isolated in my world as he was in his.

When your child is not typically developing, the reminders are ubiquitous. Every fairytale, TV commercial, and playground boasts a merciless tapestry of *normal*, that tightly woven fabric of children who are enchanting, imaginative, and *verbal*, smothering you at every turn with obvious reminders of what parenthood was supposed to mean. And so for me, parenting became an assault filled with relentless daily examples of all the ways my son was different; there was little joy, just a pervasive and haunting sense of *otherness*.

To have an autistic child is to view the world as an outsider. I watched as if from behind a wall of glass other children living life—playing "princess" and "cowboys," initiating shy introductions, negotiating ever-later bedtimes. Each taunt of *normal* delivered a swift punch to the gut because my son did not and might not ever do these things. Zack had none of the defining childlike characteristics about which parents habitually boast. *He was special in a bad way.*

When their normal children had explosive tantrums, my friends shrugged them off. They weren't terrified their child might still be throwing full-body tantrums when he turned eighteen. And all those cherished platitudes now curdled and sour: "Children say the darnedest things!" *Mine doesn't. He just yelps and screams in repetitive fits for no reason.* No, I could not gleefully chime in with friends about the outrageous statement my son just swiped me with today—my son could not even respond to his own name.

In truth, I have always been a jealous person. But I have never known a more bitter or corrosive envy than that coursing through my veins as I observed the world around me. Well-intended but foolish comments came at me constantly: "*A child is a blessing no matter what.*" Really? Even if he bites and mutilates his own flesh for no apparent reason and walks past me with the same indifference he shows a piece of furniture? "*Even with all the challenges, you would never trade your child for any other.*" Wouldn't I?

I watched numbly through a haze of tears as my son compulsively circled the perimeter of a playground in the identical pattern over and over, oblivious to the other children, to the swings and slides, to the notion of play itself. And beneath my frozen motherly façade I became lost in morbid fantasy—*if only I could slice open the skull of one of these other kids I could carve out my son's defective brain and exchange it with another child's, that one building castles in the sandbox, that one on the swing trading hysterical giggles with his father . . . I will take any child at this park regardless of personality and never look back. Just please, God, don't make me do this anymore.*

THE FALLACY OF THE CALORIE

WHY THE MODERN WESTERN DIET IS KILLING US AND HOW TO STOP IT

by Michael S. Fenster, MD

PAGES: 284

PUB DATE: 12-01-2014

SOFTCOVER: $17.95, 978-1-940192-89-5

EBOOK: $2.99, 978-1-633930-38-4

> "Dr. Fenster is a master of the presentation, both on the plate and on the page. This book should be required reading."
>
> —PROF. AMY TUCKER, MD, MHCM, FACC, Director, Club Red, UVA Heart & Vascular Center for Women

ABOUT THE BOOK

Jean Anthelme Brillat-Savarin wrote in *The Physiology of Taste*, two months before his death, "Tell me what you eat, and I will tell you who you are." In the almost two hundred years since its publication in 1825 we have borne witness to the ultimate veracity of such a simple observation.

We have seen that truism reflected in our own modern Western diet. It is a diet that delivers us unto the disabilities and diseases of modern civilization: obesity, diabetes, cardiovascular disease, gastrointestinal disease, neurologic disease, and autoimmune disease. Disabilities and diseases that have at their root a chronic, continuous low-level inflammation.

Now for the first time, Dr. Mike, cardiologist and chef, reveals the how and the why of the modern Western diet. He explains how we are hardwired to seek out sugar, salt, and fat. He details how that greed for these consumables allowed us to become the most dominant species on the planet and to construct the most technologically advanced and complex social structure the world has ever known.

But that progress has not come without a price. Dr. Mike crafts a prescription to break the vicious cycle of addiction at the heart of the modern Western diet.

ABOUT THE AUTHOR

Michael S. Fenster, MD, FACC, FSCA&I, PEMBA, known to friends and fans simply as "Dr. Mike," is America's culinary interventionalist. He is a board-certified interventional cardiologist and professional chef. He currently holds faculty cross appointments at the University of Montana College of Health Professions and Biomedical Sciences as well as the Missoula College Culinary Arts Program of the Department of Business Technology. In addition to his clinical practice, he hosts a weekly national radio show, Code Delicious with Dr. Mike, on RadioMD with podcasts available there, on iheart radio and on iTunes. He currently serves the national spokesperson for the Food as Therapy program for those suffering from neuroendocrine tumors (NETs). He has appeared as an expert guest on many national radio and television programs and has taught and explored the relationship between food and health through international workshops, seminars, lectures and cooking demonstrations. He currently writes a regular column for *Psychology Today* and has authored several books. He spends his free time between wandering the beautiful Montana mountains and the Florida Gulf; where he passively pursues his dream of a simple pirate's life.

INTRO:

This is a book for lost souls. For everyone confused by all the contradictory information out there regarding what you eat and how it affects your health; for all the people pissed off about all the nonsense that circulates as conventional wisdom; for all the people annoyed about being told that they can't have a shrimp or an egg because it's toxic with cholesterol, then finding that three years later that statement has been retracted because, "Oh geez, we guess we got that wrong. These things really are good for you. In fact they're so good for you that they are now the latest superfood. Sorry about the food substitute loaded with trans-fatty acids. Oops."

If you are easily offended, put this book down because you will be more annoyed than Jack Sparrow at an AA meeting. If you are a true believer in the conventional foodie wisdom, put this book down because it will rock that false foundation like Krakatoa. If you think the modern Western diet is a boon to mankind, put this book down because it will kick you right in your boons. If you are happy with the food you eat and how it makes you feel, your state of health and wellness, put this book down, put your hands in the air and walk away. This is not for you.

This book is for people who want to understand what has happened to our food and how it impacts our health. It is for people who want to enjoy a variety of the incredible, delicious bounty nature offers without restriction. It is for people who want to become empowered and understand the vast potential locked away in the correct balance and ratio of all the various foodstuffs we can partake of. It is for people who want some guidelines, a map upon which they can chart their own culinary journey. This book is about giving you the tools you need to understand the current state of the modern Western diet and why and what you need to change.

It is about giving you the knowledge to understand your own weaknesses to manipulation and subterfuge. That awareness gives you the power to eliminate those vulnerabilities. It is about giving you the ability to charter your own course based on solid principles founded in science; yet that can yield to your own taste and pleasure. It is written so you may enjoy both delicious, wholesome foods that bring you happiness and at the same time supply your body with the resources it needs for good health and wellness. It is about realizing that we truly are what we eat. We are a manifestation of the interaction between our genetics and our environment. The most powerful and intimate happening between these two forces occurs in our gut; mediated by a host of symbiotic bacteria.

This book is about food for nutrition, for health, for enjoyment and celebration and, perhaps most importantly, it is about food for the soul. It is about enabling you to spot the false prophets issuing a cacophony of misinformed nonsense. It is about giving you the facts to tell the shysters, self-anointed doyens and just plain ignorant know-it-all idiots to "Shut the hell up!"

Because in the deepest circles of Dante's Culinary Inferno await the most hellish health consequences.

Question everything.

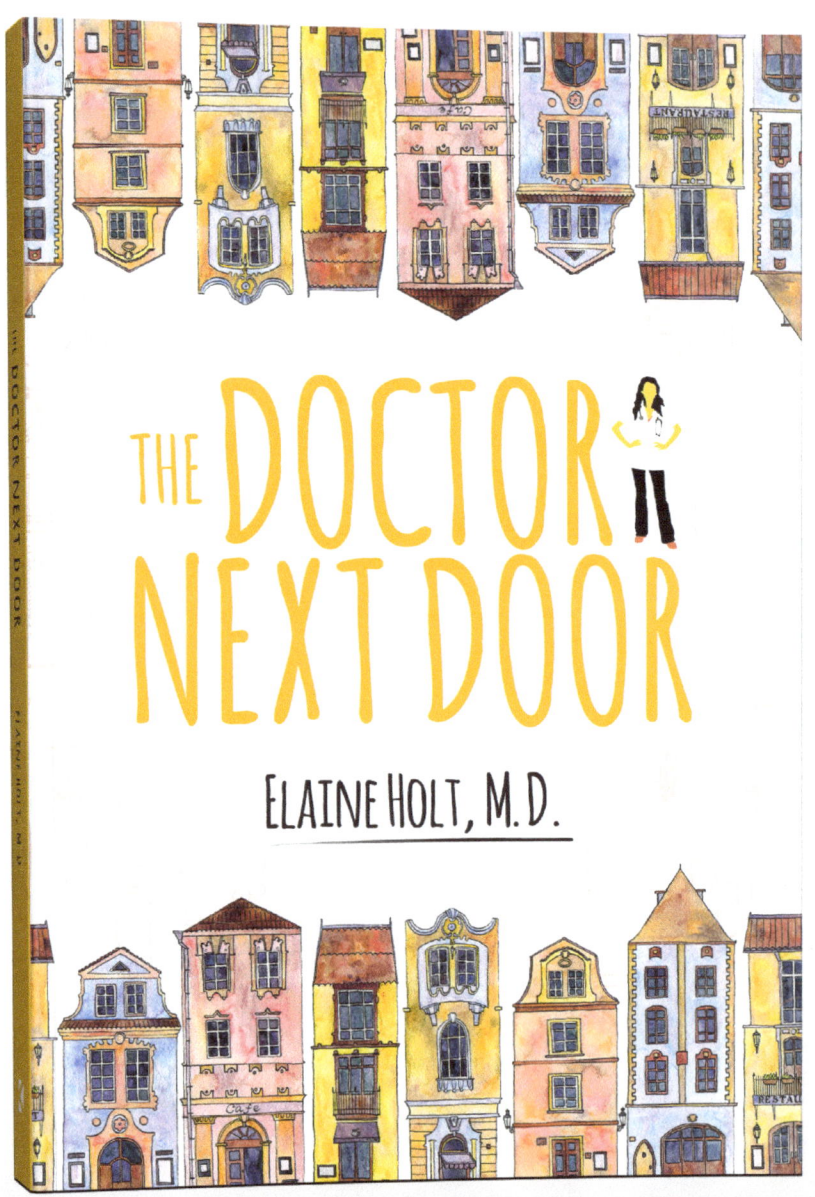

THE DOCTOR NEXT DOOR

by Elaine Holt, MD

PAGES: 190

PUB DATE: 03-21-2018

SOFTCOVER: $16.95, 978-1-63393-576-1

HARDCOVER: $25.95, 978-1-63393-578-5

"In an era of impressive but impersonal technology, Dr. Holt reminds us what is at the core of true healing: the patient/physician relationship. With inquiry, insight, and a dash of aplomb, her stories refresh the reader's spirit, and give us hope that despite the augers, the human touch will remain the heart and soul of healing."

—CHEF MICHAEL FENSTER, MD, "The Food Shaman"

ABOUT THE BOOK

Dr. Elaine Holt is not your average doctor. Her medical practice is small, while her heart for her patients is huge. *The Doctor Next Door* is a collection of extraordinary stories about ordinary people. The stories spotlight the physician as a down-to-earth person, sometimes flawed and unnervingly close to her patient's suffering. They showcase the vulnerability that both doctor and patient experience as they weave through life's challenges. *The Doctor Next Door* celebrates life, relationships, and the indomitable human spirit.

ABOUT THE AUTHOR

ELAINE HOLT, MD is a board-certified internist practicing in Ridgewood, New Jersey. She believes that a strong doctor-patient relationship is the foundation of the practice of medicine. Dr. Holt does what she loves and loves what she does as she operates her solo internal medicine practice serving her local community.

INTRODUCTION

Most doctors go into medicine with good intentions. They want to help people. I was no different. However, I had no idea that I'd end up getting as much from my patients as I'd be giving to them. You see, real medicine isn't about science. It's about people and their stories.

The Doctor Next Door is a collection of stories based on my decades of internal medicine practice. It celebrates the doctorpatient relationship, personal relationships, and the resilience of the human spirit. My hope is that these extraordinary stories of ordinary people will inspire you, as they've inspired me. As a solo practitioner swimming against the tide of corporatized medicine, I believe in the intimacy of the doctorpatient bond and I've based my career on its enduring strength.

Now, you might be wondering who I am. My patients refer to me as a modern day throwback to the small-town doctor. I was raised in a family who believed in keeping elderly relatives at home as their health, minds, and bodies declined. As a result, when it came time to assess what I wanted to be when I grew up, I had only to reflect on what I'd already become—a caregiver. I had been a "feeder" to an aging grandparent, preparing meals and spoon-feeding for as long as I can remember. Fortunately, I didn't have a naysaying guidance counselor or meddling parent telling me that my choice didn't make sense.

After completing my residency training in internal medicine in New York City, I embarked on my career as a private practice physician and have spent the last seventeen years as a custodian of patients and their stories.

A while back I found out that one of my patients, a priest, had just accepted a position at a new parish. Not knowing whether this was a promotion of sorts in his line of work, I said, "Father, congratulations on the new parish . . . It's quite a career accomplishment."

He replied, "Oh, I don't really think of it as a career. It's more like a calling, you understand."

Reflecting on my own choices, I answered, "I think I do."

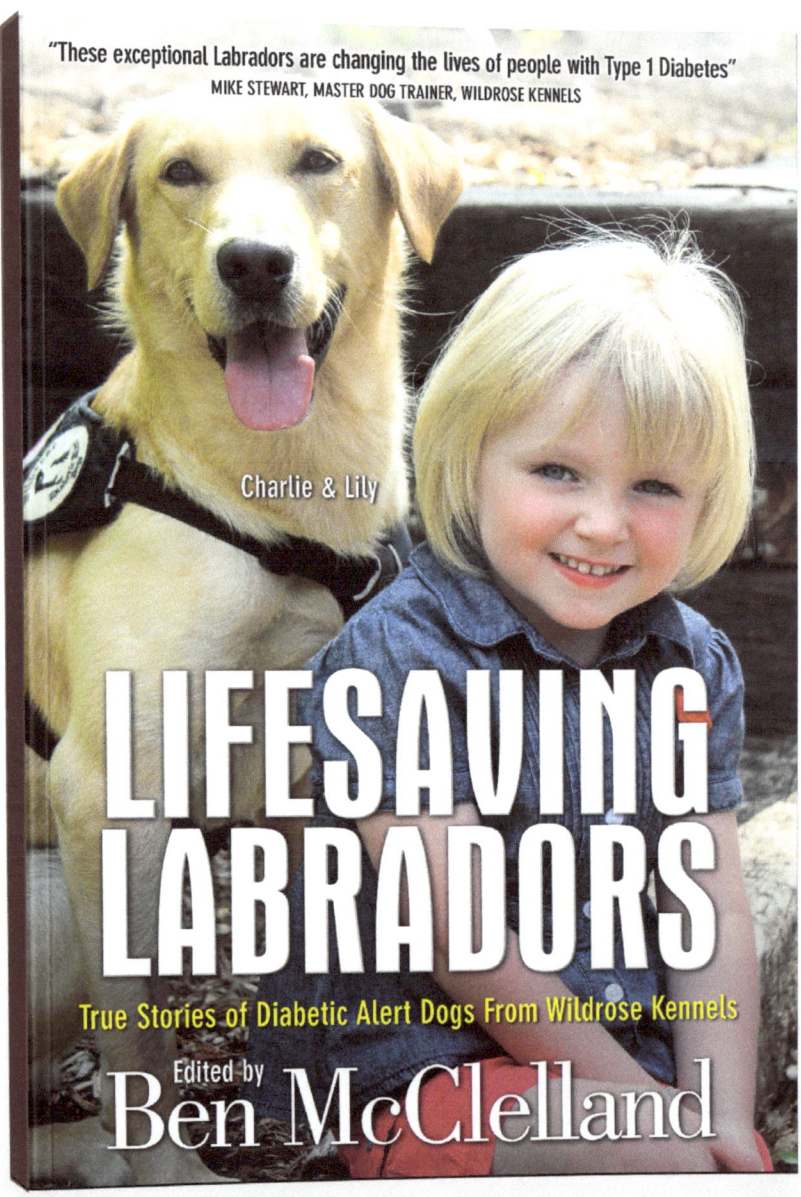

LIFESAVING LABRADORS

TRUE STORIES OF DIABETIC ALERT DOGS FROM WILDROSE KENNELS

by Ben McClelland

PAGES: 260

PUB DATE: 03-20-2014

SOFTCOVER: $17.95 978-1-93846-790-5

EBOOK: $7.49 978-1-94019-240-6

> "These exceptional Labradors are changning the lives of people with type 1 diabetes."
>
> —MIKE STEWART, Master dog trainer, Wildrose Kennels

ABOUT THE BOOK

"Diabetes is hell!" says Capri Smith, struggling with the debilitating disease that struck her daughter Ciara at age nine. Angie Simonton felt that a monster attacked her family when Lily succumbed before she was two years old. An equestrian in college, Devon Wright feared stigma and tried to shield her disease from public view. Animal EMT Megan DeHaven and Manhattan businessman Tom Arsenault worried that they would die in their sleep. Tom came to know borough EMTs by name, because he blacked out so frequently. Sharon Stinson, married and in her twenties, thought she would die like Shelby in *Steel Magnolias*. Sweet Ciara, little Lily, and the rest of the people in this book are all type 1 diabetics. Like three million other Americans they suffer from an incurable autoimmune disease that destroys the insulin-producing beta cells in the pancreas. Sugar rides a rollercoaster in each diabetic's bloodstream, sending the body into a catastrophic state. Death casts its shadow over each of them. Desperate, each one sought a diabetic alert dog from Wildrose Kennels. Known as DADs, these British Labradors use their keen sense of smell to notify the diabetic or the caregiver of low and high blood sugar levels, thereby allowing prompt corrections to avert the episode or lessen its severity. Their diabetic owners attest that their dogs save their lives—daily. *Lifesaving Labradors* explains how the dogs do it, and how they are used to change and save lives.

ABOUT THE AUTHOR

Since 2011 Ben McClelland has been associated with Wildrose Kennels as an apprentice trainer and writer of the Wildrose blog. He has also worked extensively with adults and children who have received diabetic alert dogs (DADs) from Wildrose. He is a professor and Schillig Chair of English at the University of Mississippi, where he has taught courses in literature and writing for twenty-six years. He holds a PhD in American literature from Indiana University, where he wrote a dissertation on William Faulkner's fiction. He also completed postdoctoral study at the University of Pittsburgh in composition and at Carnegie Mellon University in rhetoric. He developed professional credentials in nonfiction and life narrative writing by conducting research into the history, theory and current place of nonfiction prose in English studies. In addition to articles and editions, he has written two professional books and a nonfiction memoir, *Soldier's Son*, which was published by the University Press of Mississippi in March 2004, as a Willie Morris Book in Memoir and Biography. Since 2004 he has offered undergraduate and graduate courses in nonfiction writing. His favorite pastime is hunting with his Wildrose Labs, Eider and Mac.

INTRO

It's just a dog kennel, like some you've no doubt visited. But it's so much more. They're just ordinary folks here, like you and me. Yet there's something very different about them.

This is Mike and Cathy Stewart's Wildrose, a haven for British Labradors, tucked away in the piney hills of northern Mississippi, Faulkner's renowned landscape. Hundreds of people visit here annually to pick up pups from the celebrated genetic lines. Most are gundog enthusiasts or outdoor adventure seekers who want steady, well-trained companions at home and afield. But petite Texan Angie Simonton also visited with Lily, her blonde preschooler. College sophomore Devon Wright, a competitive equestrian, and her mother flew in from Colorado for a look. Capri Smith, a savvy romance novelist, brought daughter Ciara on an overland journey for some training with their dog, Teddy Bear. Megan DeHaven took time away from her demanding job to drive down from Ohio. Twenty-something Sharon Stinson and husband Jeremy came for Gracie. And several others like them have also visited in the last few years. Yes, these people would fit in with us at, say, a summer picnic or at a family reunion or at an afternoon concert in the park. But something significant sets them apart. Little Lily, athletic Devon, sweet Ciara, pixie-haired Megan, and Sharon, tall and demure, are all Type 1 Diabetics, an affliction that used to be known as juvenile diabetes. Like three million other Americans they suffer from an autoimmune disease that destroys the beta cells in the pancreas that are responsible for producing insulin. Death cast its shadow over each of them.

They all came to Wildrose seeking diabetic alert dogs to hold death at bay. To get here they traveled a path that pioneer Rachel Thornton had cleared for them. Rachel and her very ill eleven-year-old daughter, Abi, toughed it out, training Mr Darcy to alert for Abi. Then Rachel and Wildrose owners, Mike and Cathy Stewart, created opportunities for other diabetics and their caregivers to use dogs as medical assistants to help them monitor their levels of blood sugar (also referred to as blood glucose or BG) and live more normal lives.

Because these folks look healthy, it's hard for us to understand the medical challenges that they face every day.. Imagine that, willy-nilly, your blood sugar level could rise or fall suddenly because your pancreas no longer works to supply insulin. What's worse, you can neither predict these changes, nor can you feel any side effects—until you are dangerously sick. With a high level you might experience febrile convulsions. In the case of a low you might likely fall unconscious.

Consider the effect that this condition would have on your daily life. You could suffer an attack while swimming, riding a bike, or driving a car. You could be enjoying dinner and a movie with friends. Or you could be sound asleep in the middle of the night. Because these incidents could occur at any time and might have severe consequences, you might choose to reduce your activities and try to stay safe at home. You might become reclusive or depressed Diabetics suffer from lack of insulin production, which can lead to sudden changes in blood sugar levels. So many things contribute to sugar levels from emotions to exercise and from eating carbohydrates to getting a cold. Several times emergency responders rushed Sharon Stinson to the hospital when she fell into diabetic comas. All of the parents in this group, the around-the-clock caregivers for their children, have frantically administered Glucagon shots or force-fed sugar drinks in desperate attempts to steady erratic glycemic events. Like Capri Smith, all of them have gone on daredevil car rides to the ER, desperate to save their daughters' lives. "Battling diabetes is an unimaginable fight. Every day," Kitty Berry attests "The fight requires every bit of energy and faith we can muster."

Monitoring blood sugar levels is an unrelenting task for Type 1 diabetics and their caregivers. The goal is to maintain tight control over the glycemic range, minimizing fluctuations so as to maintain normal activities and to prevent any of the several harmful side effects of wide, erratic sugar swings. Even with modern insulin monitoring and delivery systems, Type 1 Diabetics continue to struggle to achieve healthy monthly averages, a key to long-term health.

A diabetic alert dog, known as a DAD, is a tool in diabetes management. Each dog is trained to notify the diabetic or the caregiver of low and high blood sugar levels, thereby allowing them to promptly make necessary corrections to avert the episode or lessen its severity. A hypo- or hyperglycemic attack can lead to a seizure, coma, or death, making these well-trained dogs true lifesavers. The DAD's performance can result in tighter glycemic control, which decreases the likelihood of devastating, long-term complications, including kidney failure, retinopathy, neuropathy, and heart disease.

As these diabetics and their caregivers struggled with this relentless disease, they turned to dogs as effective monitors of blood sugar changes. Mr Darcy, Teddy Bear, Olive, Gracie, Ruby, Charlie, Keeper, Willow, Juniper, Drake, and Hatch—these canines are the masters of scent, the heroes of their owners' real-life dramas. These DADs consistently alert their owners to sugar level changes more frequently and sooner than the mechanical monitors that the diabetics wear. Some report that dog alerts are twenty minutes ahead of the monitors; some, as much as an hour ahead. What do these precious minutes mean to the diabetic or her caregiver? In the case of rapidly falling blood levels, it can enable one to take preventive action to head off a precipitous drop before it plunges dangerously low.

How does the dog monitor changes in blood sugar level? When some people first hear about diabetic alert dogs, they are in awe at the dogs' ability to "smell." Others are skeptical. Dr. Dana Hardin, of Eli Lilly and Company, is conducting research into the special scenting abilities of DADs to discover scientific evidence of the volatile organic compounds that dogs may smell emanating from a diabetic's body in, for example, perspiration, breath, and saliva. We have long known that dogs possess a superior olfactory system. Relying on dogs' keen scenting capabilities, trainers have employed dogs to seek out numerous things from cached drugs and lost hikers to shed antlers and arson accelerants. Just as hunting dogs are trained to follow the scent of wild game and drug-detection dogs are trained to sniff out concealed illegal drugs, DADs are trained to smell changes in human scent when a diabetic's blood sugar level changes. Current research on canine olfaction reveals a complex, sophisticated method of knowing the world by smell. Dogs know us primarily by smell, using extensive nasal passages and odor-collection chambers, as well as the nasal vomeronasal organ, a special sac "covered with more receptor sites for molecules." Dogs recognize us by our unique odors—by our sweat, perfume, and clothing. They can tell if we've just bathed and what food or drink we've recently had. And as our storywriters reveal, DADs smell, sense, know their team members' sugar levels.

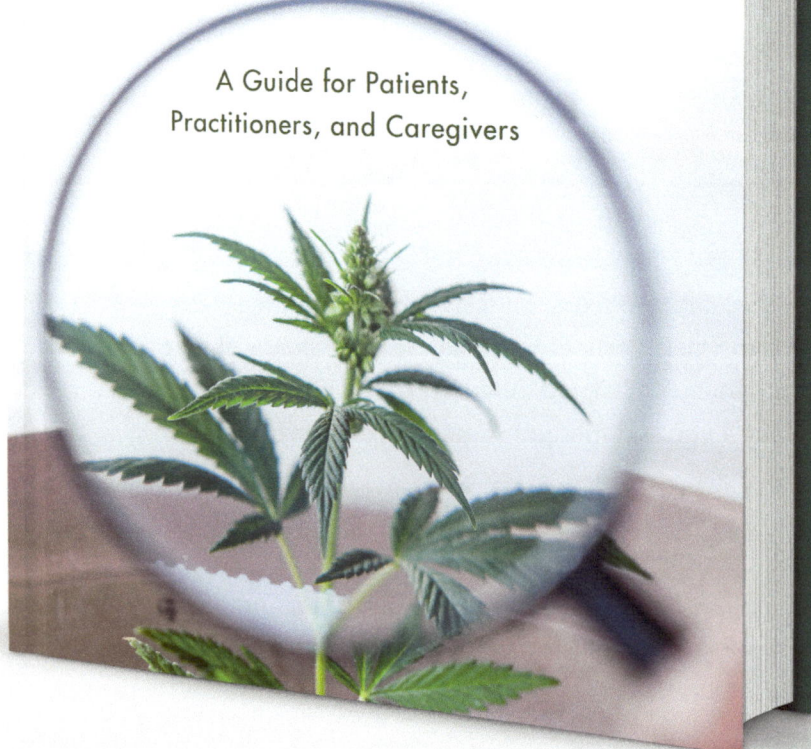

MEDICAL CANNABIS

A GUIDE FOR PATIENTS, PRACTITIONERS, AND CAREGIVERS

by Michael H. Moskowitz, MD, MPH

PAGES: 236

PUB DATE: 11-30-2017

SOFTCOVER: $24.95, 978-1-63393-538-9

HARDCOVER: $34.95, 978-1-63393-540-2

EBOOK: $9.99, 978-1-63393-539-6

> "... a vital discourse on the subject for patients and medical professionals alike."
>
> — JOSÉ J. HIDALGO, Founder & CEO Knox Medical

ABOUT THE BOOK

Can Medical Cannabis help you? Forty-four states and the District of Columbia have legalized some form of medical cannabis for treatment of serious conditions. Pain, cancer, sleep disturbance, mood disorders, epilepsy, osteoporosis, anxiety disorders, and many others are all conditions that may be helped by this treatment. Author Dr. Michael Moskowitz reviews the science of our own built in cannabinoid system, then launches into practical topics, including medical cannabis treatment, dispensary management, paraphernalia, embodiments, routes of administration, and DIY treatment. He covers the complexities of state laws, learning the phases of treatment, working with dispensaries, understanding the different embodiments and routes of administration, knowing how to avoid undesirable psychotropic effects, and combining this approach with both traditional and alternative medical care. The book details many ways of using this treatment without being cognitively altered.

It is meticulously documented, and scientifically grounded to both help physicians with recommendations and treatment planning and in delivering highly relevant and useful treatment choices for patients. Whether you are a patient, practitioner, caregiver or lawmaker, *Medical Cannabis: A Guide for Patients, Practitioners, and Caregivers* separates myth from reality and proves itself invaluable to your own decision making about this therapeutic approach.

ABOUT THE AUTHOR

Michael H. Moskowitz, MD, MPH is a board-certified physician in both Psychiatry and Pain Medicine. He is the co-author of the *Neuroplastic Transformation Workbook* and the neuroplastix.com website. The Neuroplastic Transformation Workbook has been sold in over fifty countries around the world. The website is the number one searched website in the world on neuroplastic treatment. The author has articles published in multiple peer-reviewed medical journals and several peer-reviewed textbook chapters. Dr. Moskowitz was an assistant professor of pain medicine in the anesthesiology department of University of California, Davis, Medical Center, Davis for twelve years, where he taught courses on the neuroplasticity of pain and on medical cannabis for the treatment of pain. He has also taught about medical cannabis at the University of California, San Francisco annual spine conferences, the American Academy of Pain Medicine annual national conferences and Walter Reed Army Hospital at the Military and VA Annual International Pain Skills Conference. He is a also a practicing physician at Bay Area Pain Medical Associates in San Rafael, California, in the San Francisco Bay Area, where he treats many of his persistent pain patients with medical cannabis.

INTRODUCTION

The purpose of this book is to help people with serious illness and their caregivers, providers and their patients and legislators and their constituents to understand the issues involved in making medical cannabis available as treatment for people who have the potential to benefit from it. This is not a simple issue of legalizing medical cannabis. It is woven as deeply into the fabric of our society as health and illness and civil disobedience. Denying it has led to the failed war on drugs, development of an underground economy, a clash of states' rights versus federalism, criminalization of marginalized members of society, racial inequality, and the incarceration of millions of people for recreational and medical use. It provides an alternative to standard care and hope for the hopeless. This is a true grassroots issue that seemed to come out of nowhere, demanding social justice for the seriously ill.

While the current state of the law is fragmented, and unjust, offering availability to some, and the threat of prison to others, it is also a tentative start of a medical revolution. Although there is some excellent and well-researched science on the subject, clinical application is confusing and clinical science lags behind basic research, pharmacological science, and clinical availability. This guide is meant to be interactive and to explain the scope of this treatment, which is varied and quite effective for many. It involves both potential palliation and cure for many conditions. It opens avenues for traditional drug development and plant refinement to solve some of the more stubborn clinical problems that linger to this day. Medical cannabis does not, however, rely on that scientific development. It transcends modern medical treatment, in favor of compassionate use of a plant that anyone can grow and use. Wending through the myriad issues involved in making this treatment work requires information and advice that integrates it into overall medical care. Doctors who certify patients should be aware of the benefits and side effects of various phytocannabinoids present in cannabis. People who choose this treatment need support and advice, from their physicians and other health professionals. Even experienced and successful users can gain new insights that point to new directions in treatment decision making. Informed lawmakers can use increased knowledge to make more reasonable laws that help people get more access to the care they need, while protecting the public's safety. Greater understanding of the issues can lead society to improve its treatment of those in need, including people who have been incarcerated for a substance that others now use to improve their physical and mental health. Mostly, this guide is dedicated to helping those who now suffer to instead live and thrive.

Medical cannabis is not your father's Mary Jane. This is a treatment that is quite different from recreational cannabis. The focus of care is to learn how to use cannabis without feeling high, but this does not mean that the main psychoactive component, THC, should be avoided. It is an important, highly pharmacological part of the Total Cannabinoid Profile (TCP) of the plant and a useful aspect of using medical cannabis. The treatment can never be accurately evaluated with the standard for traditional medical research, but the need for excellent research remains critical. Such research has been in the hands of the people, backed by the states that have challenged the federal authorities. Physicians and researchers must be free to study its effects within strains, between strains, while mixing and matching strains, embodiments and various delivery systems. Its use is supported through all age groups, across political and religious beliefs, and among people with a broad range of medical conditions. Its use for pain, anxiety, and sleep can be superior to current medications, and the whole plant ensemble effect is more therapeutic than individually extracted, pure components. Medical cannabis is helpful in lowering the use of other medications, including opioids, and can substitute for them or work with them, helping optimize medication use to the lowest possible dose. Recent studies have shown cannabis components to not only treat numerous brain degenerative disorders, including Alzheimer's disease, but to also slow down the normal cognitive decline of aging

Cannabis has been used by people for at least the last five millennia. History of its medical use dates to before 1000 BC. This use came to a crashing end in the 1940s, when United States Attorney General Harry Anslinger banned its use with a Catch 22-esque tax law, and threatened to immediately jail any physician who tried to use it in patient care. This was all reinforced decades later, when marijuana was given schedule 1 status, putting it in the same class as heroin, methamphetamine, and crack cocaine. The subsequent war on drugs not only reinforced the nefarious status of marijuana, but resulted in jail and prison time for many people around the world. In the United States, according to statistics from the ACLU, more than half of drug arrests are for possession of marijuana, and a person of color has a 3.72 more likely chance of being arrested for marijuana possession. Even more surprising, between 2001 and 2010, 88 percent of the 8.2 million arrests for marijuana crimes were for simple possession. The US Government and many others have spawned an atmosphere of fear mongering, biased "scientific" research, propaganda, and racial inequality. Ultimately this has resulted in one of the most medically useful plants ever known, being deemed without medical value.

Research has been very limited in the United States. In the 1930s, there was a flurry of research into the chemistry of cannabis in the US, Britain, and Germany, leading to the discovery of cannabidiol (CBD) and cannabinol (CBN) and their isolation from the plant in pure form. This research determined the chemical structure of CBD and developed a few synthetic cannabinoids before it went dark from the 1940s to the 1960s. In the 1960s, Israeli researchers Mechoulam, Shvo, and Gaoni determined several of the properties and components of plant-based cannabis, leading, in the 1980s and 1990s, to the discovery of the innate endocannabinoid system in humans. Their work launched the modern understanding of the medical importance of our built-in cannabinoid system.

NEW ADHD MEDICATION RULES

BRAIN SCIENCE & COMMON SENSE

by Dr. Charles Parker

PAGES: 180

PUB DATE: 01-01-2013

SOFTCOVER: $14.95   978-1-93846-722-6

EBOOK: $6.99   978-1-93846-734-9

ABOUT THE BOOK

New ADHD Medication Rules deals with the over-medication, missed diagnoses and imbalanced medical treatments used today in the treatment of ADHD. Dr. Parker shows where and how these imbalances occur, provides the data and explanations for why treatment is often incorrect, and then simplifies and explains insightful methods for dealing with ADHD medications, both for medical practioners and parents of kids and adults with ADHD. *Rules* is based upon the latest brain science, and includes a variety of associated treatment topics that address the real complexity of ADHD medical management. The variables that effect medication effectiveness range from sleep, to breakfast, to biomedical interferences that can dramatically change the way medications burn in the body. Without *Rules* the possibility of missing potentially dangerous drug interactions and associated diagnostic challenges, such as depression and anxiety, adds to the greater possibility of treatment failure.

ABOUT THE AUTHOR

Dr. Charles Parker is a writer (*Deep Recovery, ADHD Medication Rules*, CorePsych Blog), a neuroscientist certified for SPECT brain imaging, and a practicing child and adult psychiatrist with more than forty-three years of experience in clinical practice. From psychoanalysis to psychopharmacology, Parker brings a unique perspective and passion to the changes that must be made in the current diagnostic and treatment protocols for psychiatric conditions in general, and ADHD most specifically. He knows the territory not only from direct experience with active practice clients, but from those many years, since '96, lecturing to medical colleagues on the science and applications of psychotropic meds for several pharma companies. His cutting-edge interest in the dramatic advances in molecular and cellular physiology associated with effective brain function teach professionals and clients at every level about cognitive and emotional imbalance. Parker's mission is compelling and persuasive: brain science translation into common sense packages for everyday use. His CorePsych Blog has won numerous ADHD writing awards over the years, and set new standards for the diagnosis and treatment of executive function disorders. Dr. Parker works and lives in Virginia Beach, Virginia.

INTRODUCTION

Pills have to pass through your body before they reach your brain. The body is uniformly overlooked. What happens along that complex journey determines a drug's effectiveness and predictability.

Unfortunately, far too many significant problems exist with Attention Deficit Hyperactivity Disorder meds because those who prescribe them don't consider or grasp the ways drugs are absorbed and then processed in the bowel, liver or the brain itself. A patient's diet, medical status and allergies are given only modest consideration. The interactions of multiple medications also are given short shrift. Instead, physicians often base dosages on broad –- even vague -- medication formulas. Too many prescribe from statistical averages, not individual needs.

Succinctly: too many simply are not paying attention to the meds for paying attention.

What I hope to accomplish through this book is to enlighten my medical colleagues and embolden patients suffering with ADHD or symptoms masquerading as an attention or hyperactivity disorder. My intention is to arm patients, or those caring for them, with enough critical information to at least ask their doctors informed questions and challenge limited conventional thinking.

Much of the information presented here is highly scientific. Some of it is anecdotal, and the rest is clearly advocacy. It's my firm belief, after spending decades treating those struggling with emotional and mental illnesses, that treatments should be customized based upon available science. Most importantly, physicians and patients need to partner in treatments so that medications can be adjusted correctly.

The wrong mix of drugs or prescriptions in the wrong amounts can be deadly. They can tip someone with depression into suicide. They can exacerbate, rather than alleviate, hyperactivity. The wrong blends or amounts of drugs can harm rather than heal.

ADHD diagnosis and treatment strategies are tricky to begin with. Technology has advanced to a point where it's now possible to read the brain's reaction to drugs and to find in the body root causes for previously unpredictable problems. Yet, too few physicians are willing or capable of employing these new assessment techniques. Treatments are not on a par with current, easily available brain science, leaving a global quandary about viable ADHD practice strategies.

ADHD medications don't work like slap shots in a penny arcade. They must be exact with laser accuracy to hit their intended targets. Too many with ADHD are treated with cookie-cutter medication recipes and diagnoses based upon superficial behavioral appearances that overlook the complexity of the human brain. What's missing is applied neuroscience discoveries; years of brain scan data and biomedical evidence should drive more effective diagnosis and medication delivery.

My hope is that *New New ADHD Medication Rules* raises awareness of better and more sophisticated approaches to treating and diagnosing ADHD.

WHY RULES AND WHY ME?

I've witnessed medical denial all over the country. After speaking nationally to thousands of doctors, nurses and mental health professionals since first starting to practice in the 1970s, I've come to important conclusions: Too many don't want to listen to the neuroscience data; too many are focused on those superficial, often counterproductive DSM 4/5 labels;

too many docs hurry to prescribe ADHD meds without considering real consequences.

Regrettably, some of the most pressing medical denial and defensive, self-righteous thinking exists in otherwise sophisticated metropolitan communities with the most prestigious medical academic institutions. Ironically, some of the most intelligent and otherwise well-informed communities, such as Boston, New York City and San Francisco, shun new medical information unless it comes from their in-town provincial, group-think establishment thought leaders.

I've watched their responses to my presentations over the years, and repeatedly experienced their determined resistance to thoughtful investigation and improved intervention strategies. Intellectual egoism rules, serves to neglect critical thinking, and shrouds progress in wrappings of doctrinaire beliefs that don't match biomedical brain evidence. The outcome of these blinders is that you, the patient, from New York to South Africa, suffer the consequences of ineffective or potentially dangerous treatments.

EXPERIENCE MATTERS

In a word, *Rules* arises from more than forty years of practice feedback from patients, especially when I didn't get the meds right following the most approved protocols. I listened, and I looked for additional answers and more evidence-based approaches. *Rules* summarizes that learning history.

I've repeatedly interviewed thousands of clients who suffered for years at the hands of denial and medical innocence. After a hasty diagnostic process, too few medical providers show interest in expectations of how the meds work in the first place, or how they should work most effectively in the long run. For example, many think understanding interactions between stimulants and other medications is a waste of time and inconsequential, despite the fact that it can result in suicidal thinking.

Repeated clinical experiences provoked me to reveal to the public, specifically ADHD sufferers, the dangers and shortcomings of the status quo and its dated practices.

My hope is that *Rules* stimulates patients and conscientious medical practitioners to improve the consideration of treatment alternatives. ADHD dogma will be exposed and public sentiment will hopefully encourage individual challenges to the current medical establishment. By reading *Rules,* I hope you will become one of the informed who will ultimately pressure treatment providers to break from mainstream thinking and adapt more comprehensive ADHD diagnosis and treatment options. Let's work together to encourage a revolution in awareness that will mandate reforms to the way medical professionals evaluate and treat this disorder.

M. GAZI YASARGIL

FATHER OF MODERN NEUROSURGERY

by Larry Rogers, MD

PAGES: 546

PUB DATE: 08-22-2015

SOFTCOVER: $24.95, 978-1-63393-113-8

HARDCOVER: $36.95, 978-1-63393-182-4

EBOOK: $8.99, 978-1-63393-114-5

> "An interesting, praise-worthy biography of a famous, praise-worthy man."
>
> —DUKE STANSON, M.D., Chairman emeritus, Department of Neurological Surgey Texas-Southwestern, Dallas

ABOUT THE BOOK

Gazi Yasargil: Father of Modern Neurosurgery is an account of a famous man's unusual and inspiring life, particularly as a youth in the first 138 pages of the book. Later, as a neurosurgeon, he found a means of reducing the mortality rates associated with the deadliest of brain pathologies from 30 percent in the mid-1960s to less than 2 percent. It required not only a vastly redesigned microscope, but an array of new surgical instruments, even a new way of thinking. 1967 witnessed neurosurgeons flocking to Zurich from around the world to learn his method. Yasargil possessed a truly amazing surgical talent, but his brand of microneurosurgery allowed even the lesser skilled to achieve stunning results if the requisite laboratory-hours to master the method were observed. Yasargil's life and times were as dramatic and challenging as microneurosurgery was important.

ABOUT THE AUTHOR

Larry Rogers learned the rudiments of microneurosurgery under the tutelage of his subject, Professor Gazi Yasargil, while visiting Switzerland as a fourth-year resident from the University of Texas Southwestern Medical School in Dallas. His undergraduate degree was from Davidson College and he graduated from the Duke Medical School. Ultimately he practiced microneurosurgery in Charlotte, North Carolina, for twenty-seven years. He has authored or co-authored four additional books, three of which are about microneurosurgery, including a novel set in the 1980s. He is married to a wonderful lady and has produced six adult children, including three daughters (an obstetrician-gynecologist, a major-league baseball writer, and one who has produced two special grandsons) plus three sons (a college professor and two computer entrepreneurs, one of whom has produced two beautiful, precious daughters; the other is deceased, but his memory remains very special indeed). In the fall, his day job is coaching high school football players.

PREFACE

"Let us now praise famous men, and our Fathers that begat us."
Ecclesiastics 44:1 (1611 KJB)

As is true with many surgical disciplines, the short developmental history of neurological surgery is the story of the wisdom, talent and fortitude of a small number of pioneer surgeons whose gifts to medicine far surpass their own technical virtuosity. These few giants are the true fathers of our specialty, and since the time of Harvey Cushing, no individual has personally dominated the evolution of neurological surgery as has Mahmud Gazi Yasargil.

Beginning in the late 1960s, Professor Yasargil has directly influenced the career of each practicing neurosurgeon, and through them the health and well-being of millions of surgical patients. This feat would be a remarkable accomplishment for any young physician emerging from the hallowed ivy towers of Europe or America; that it was accomplished by an impoverished young Turkish medical student who arrived in war-weary Germany during the final months of the Second World War is almost beyond belief. This is that incredible story.

Dr Larry Rogers, a retired neurosurgeon and well-published author, studied briefly with Yasargil in Zurich during 1973. Stunned by the conceptual and technical revolution Yasargil brought to operative neurosurgery on a daily basis, Rogers subsequently watched that revolution sweep through academic medical centers and private surgical clinics alike, ultimately to become the standard of world-wide neurosurgical practice. In less than a decade, a specialty previously wedded to incremental change saw itself fundamentally transformed in a quantum leap powered by the insight and courage of this single surgeon. From Dr. Rogers' unique prospective as a former student, a surgical practitioner and a personal acquaintance, he is uniquely qualified to document the life, times, and influence of this seminal figure.

Mahmud Gazi Yasargil is a multi-faceted, intriguing individual whose personality has evoked a broad spectrum of interactions during his dramatic rise and subsequent reign as the world's most famous neurosurgeon. The nature and scope of those interactions are integral to a clear understanding of both the man and his surgical genius . Their complexity contributes important texture, color, and contrast to this admirable portrait of the 'Father of Modern Neurosurgery.'

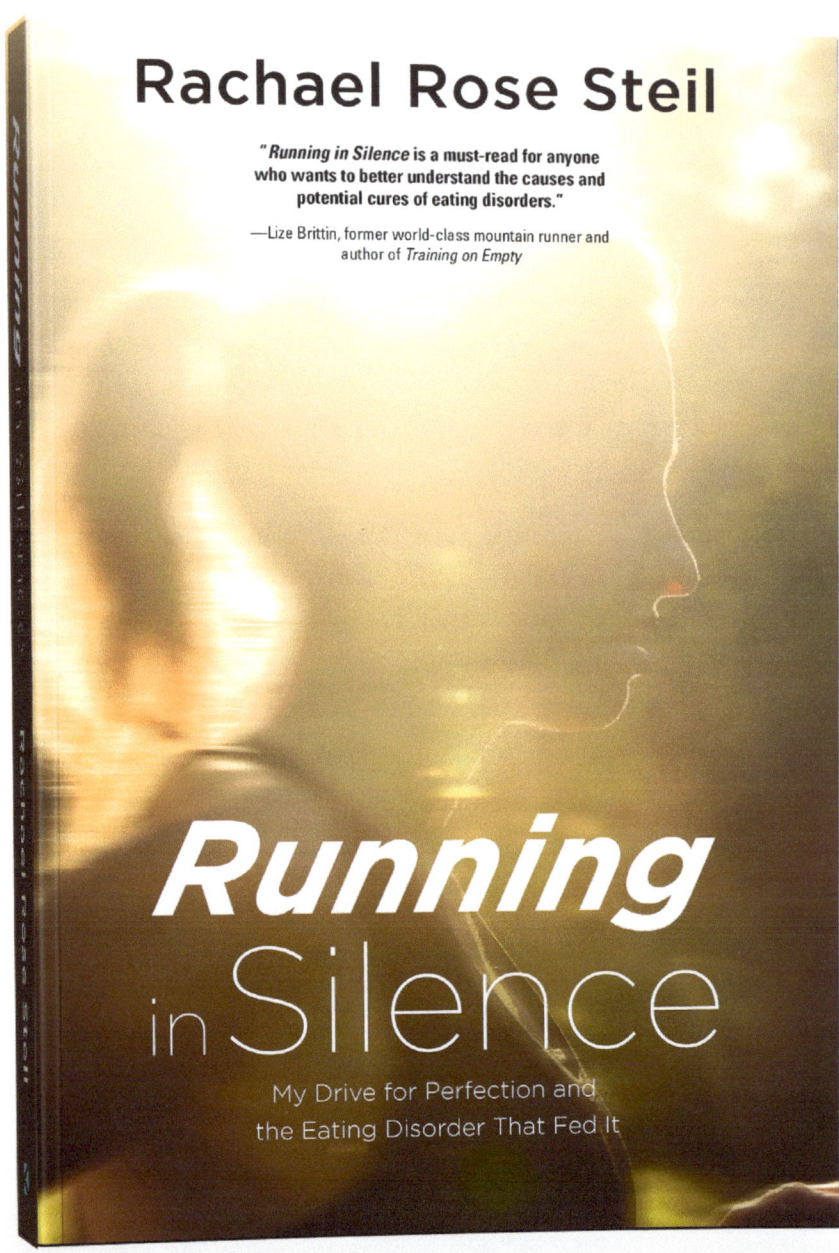

RUNNING IN SILENCE

MY DRIVE FOR PERFECTION AND THE EATING DISORDER THAT FED IT

by Rachael Rose Steil

PAGES: 346

PUB DATE: 11-15-2016

SOFTCOVER: $19.95 978-1-63393-340-8

EBOOK: $4.99 978-1-63393-341-5

> "*Running in Silence* is a must-read for anyone who wants to better understand the causes and potential cures of eating disorders."
>
> —LIZE BRITTIN, former world-class mountain runner and author of *Training on Empty*

ABOUT THE BOOK

"It had been hours since I ran at track practice that winter, but I hadn't bothered to shower let alone change clothes. No, I didn't have time for that, because I had found the answer to my prayers. This has to be it. Eat all the fruit you want. Never get fat. Raw. Food. Diet."

Rachael Steil clocked in as an all-American collegiate runner; she became a girl clawing for a comeback on a thirty-bananas-a-day diet. This year-long struggle with raw food ended when she realized she had to find her self-respect beyond her identity as a successful runner on a perfect diet. *Running in Silence* opens the door on the secret world of eating disorders. It provides vital insights for those who don't suffer from this disease and an honest and harrowing personal story for those who do. Steil challenges the stigma of eating disorders, looks past appearance, and dives into the heart of obsession.

ABOUT THE AUTHOR

Rachael Rose Steil graduated in 2015 from Aquinas College with a bachelor of arts in English. She is a level 1 USA track-and-field certified coach and is currently the assistant coach at Grandville High School. She has published articles about running and eating disorders in *Michigan Runner* magazine and is a speaker and advocate. Steil is a recipient of the Spirit and Outstanding Runner award for the Aquinas College cross-country team and has received sixth-place all-American accolades in cross country, as well as seventh place in the NAIA track nationals. Yet her greatest achievement was not breaking a physical barrier, but a mental one.

INTRODUCTION

With a butter knife in one hand and the numbers on a scale in the other, I pulled the crumbs and rock-hard frosting of the frozen birthday cake up to my tongue.

And I clawed. I clawed deeper into the cake from my squatting position over the chilly kitchen floor, clawed desperately for any morsel I could chip off the solid block of sugar. All the while the hair on the back of my neck stood up for fear that someone would come by and catch me in the act, for fear that someone would walk into this cold, white kitchen and find good, sweet Rachael sitting before the open door of the refrigerator as a food thief.

I could have waited for the cake to thaw. I could have pulled the cover off the dessert to avoid cutting my wrist as my hand scrambled beneath the plastic. In fact, you could say that with proper discipline and control I could have avoided the incident altogether.

Only, I *had* been the epitome of discipline for the past two years. The girl who snuck into the desolate kitchen that night couldn't even recognize herself when she frantically opened all the cabinets and drawers only to find them bare, when she pulled at her face with desperation and want. The girl who had been eating cooked food all day when she seemed so adamant about her raw food *lifestyle* could barely believe she was now putting not just her *purity* in jeopardy, but also her running success. Nonetheless, she opened that refrigerator door to find the frozen cake sitting before her like a god on its chilly throne.

All-American.

I slammed the blunt knife into the stiff icing.

School record-holder.

Brown cake crumbs scattered everywhere.

Raw. Food. Runner.

I grabbed a chunk of frosting between my shaking fingers, all the while knowing this was not the first time I was putting my newest, greatest running career at stake. I could already imagine the confusion on my parents' faces when I crossed the finish line of the 5k in over eighteen minutes; how my teammates would shake their heads and mutter something about "her raw food diet" and the skeptical eyes that would trail up and down my growing body, how upsetting it would be to reveal the Rachael I had tried to push down for so long, the Rachael my new college friends and coaches never saw because I entered collegiate cross country and track with a body shrunken from my high school one—a body now equipped with a dark voice whispering its incantations, its reminders of how different I was, how I needed to exert more control because *something was broken inside of me.*

And as I continued to reach for the cake that night, as I repeatedly told myself, *This is the last nibble, this is the last piece of frosting.*

I could feel the walls of the hallway just outside the kitchen closing in on me, tighter and tighter.

Someone is coming.

They will find you.

You will grow bigger.

You must stop this.

The very air suffocated me, fear electrified my body, and the lights of the small kitchen glared down at me until the butter knife slipped.

The knife slipped from my frosting-covered fingers and clanked to the floor. And I jumped, my heart pounding wildly as I wondered who could have heard, who would come running in and how I could possibly explain what the hell I was doing.

But the hallway outside the kitchen remained as silent as ever. And deciding this was a good chance to escape before anyone did come, I let the refrigerator door fall shut, slid my foot across the tile floor to remove all evidence of cake-thievery, and dashed back to my room.

The dark voice followed. It swept through the hallway with me, clung to my shoulder as I entered the guest room and realized with horror what I had done. Because the moment I entered the bathroom and looked down at the chocolate cake crumbs peppering my outstretched palms, my mind was screaming.

Calories.

Binger.

Thief.

I struggled to turn on the faucet, my fingers slipping with frosting residue, but not even the rush of cold water could flood out the voice. I tried to reassure myself that this mistake was fine because it meant I had come to a breaking point, and I promised everything would change from here.

But it was a promise I kept breaking that summer. Because even as I washed my hands vigorously, even as I promised again and again that this was the last time, the Rachael deep down burned with a passion, a hunger, a desperation that the raw food diet could not fix.

* * *

In November of 2010, a year before this scene in the kitchen, I took sixth at the national cross country meet of the National Association of Intercollegiate Athletics (NAIA). I was fast, but I was not fast enough to win. At about the same time, a friend told me about what I later found to be the miracle diet for athletes. It was the raw food diet, and it had become all the rage for the most disciplined, health-conscious athletes, athletes, I thought, like me. Better yet, I knew I was perhaps the only college runner to take on something as daring as this.

But this raw food choice was more than just a new way of eating; it promised to solve all my problems with food and all my unhappiness. It did neither.

Running in Silence began as a series of journal entries when I first started focusing seriously on my weight and investigating all the different diets that promised success. At some point, I realized that my story was more than just my story and that by writing about the specific ways in which I got free of the trap of disordered eating, I could help other runners and people in general.

I came through my own eating disorder, and I want to tell others how that happened. It is intended as a study guide that will be most effective if you consider the questions labeled "Food for Thought" about each chapter and then let the "Mile Markers" guide you toward understanding and healing a possible eating disorder or addiction in your own life. You should also make full use of the worksheets at the back of the book.

The greatest lesson I learned in this long and confusing journey was that my body was never broken, my mind was never beyond repair, and I was never really as alone as I thought I was. You are part of my story, and I want you to share the same ending I did—that of recovery, redemption, and hope.

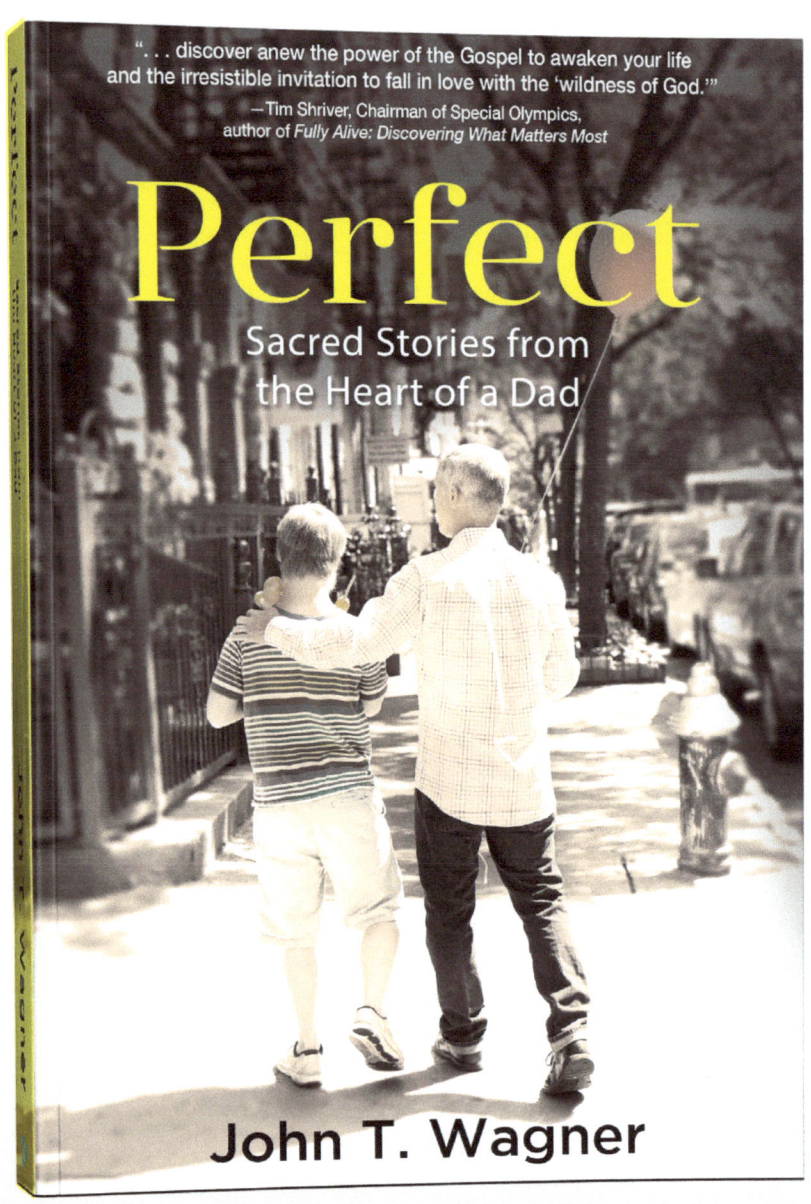

PERFECT
STORIES FROM THE HEART OF A DAD

by John T. Wagner

PAGES: 232

PUB DATE: 12-07-2016

SOFTCOVER: $14.95, 978-1-63393-198-5

HARDCOVER: $24.95, 978-1-63393-200-5

EBOOK: $4.99, 978-1-63393-199-2

> "... discover anew the power of the Gospel to awaken your life and the irresistible invitation to fall in love with the 'wildness of God.'"
>
> —TIM SHRIVER, chairman of Special Olympics, author of *Fully Alive: Discovering What Matters Most*

ABOUT THE BOOK

In our world, David will never be able to "earn it." He'll never make a lot of money. He'll never be "important." He'll never have a "big job" or own his own home. By any measure in our society and culture, he won't be "successful."

But you can't get that boy off the dance floor. He's not self-conscious. He doesn't so much think or care about who's looking at him. He doesn't need your approval. At all.

He is fully aware, fully in tune, completely swallowed up by the fact, the absolute fact, that he is loved. And he knows it. And it just flows out of him. Out of every pore of his being.

In *Perfect*, author John T. Wagner tells the stories of his son David, a seventeen-year-old boy with Down syndrome, and how David has led him more fully to the sacred stories of Jesus. Get ready to dance, laugh, cry, celebrate, wonder, treasure, believe and be wrapped in pure joy as you meet this little boy who is precious to the Savior and a gift to all those around him.

ABOUT THE AUTHOR

John Wagner is a senior vice president with Young Life and has been David's dad for the last seventeen years. He has watched his son grow and struggle. David has taught him more than he can ever talk about or write in a book about what it means to follow Jesus, but he has made the attempt to capture a small piece of that. John has a BA from Wake Forest University and an masters of divinity from Fuller Seminary. He has been on Young Life staff for thirty-three years and is currently located in New York City with his beautiful wife, Gae, and their three kids, Michael, Jessi, and David. John Wagner is also an ordained minister in the Presbyterian Church.

INTRO

Gae and I were driving to North Carolina to see my brother and his family. We were somewhere between Durham and Greensboro on I-40, driving sleepily along with our two beautiful kids, a boy and a girl, our cute little dog, and our fairly new, recently purchased mid-sized minivan, me with my gorgeous, blond Texan wife, she with me, and "Hootie" cranking on the cassette, hurtling down the road towards Asheville, NC. I had just been promoted at work, we had bought a nice brick, four-bedroom, hardwoodfloor, working-fireplace, big-back-porch house set in the city with a yard and room for a swing. Ministry was booming. We loved our church. Life was good, real good, almost perfect. Why mess that up? We're good. Check. Check. Check. Done.

The year was 1995.

Gae and I had had this conversation before. For those of you who are married, you realize the importance of timing. Some things need to wait, to marinate. Other things, you just need to move on. It had been maybe six months since I had brought this up. It went nowhere. Complete dud. I had dropped it. Figured we just weren't ready.

But this day felt different. I felt good. I felt lucky. I felt some movement. Connected. Oneness. Positive. Sense of direction. Mojo. Maybe God was truly with me this time. Maybe stars were aligning. Maybe I had some flow that wasn't with me the last time.

So I did. I just blurted it out. "What do you think about having another kid, a baby?" There it was. As a guy and an extravert, I am uncomfortable with silence. I look to fill the air. I want to keep talking, explain myself, see different sides and angles, perspectives. Work on a timeline. Problem solve. I did none of that. I just let it out and let it lay there. Like a big egg. And waited.

"I'd be open to that," she said.

"Huh? What? What did you say?" I almost wrecked the car. Our lives are perfect. Why would we want to mess that up? Why would we want another kid? We have two, one of each—they are gorgeous, perfect. We are just hitting our stride. We have momentum. Life is good, real good.

I won't bore you with the details, but it took us over two years to get pregnant. We had one miscarriage and some complications in between. But then, one day in early September, that little pink stick turned blue, or the little blue stick turned pink, or whatever it does, and Gae looked at me and said, "I'm pregnant." And we laughed, we cried, we hugged, we held hands. We were good. We were happy. We were nervous, but we were happy.

Preparations for a third child are not like preparations for a first child. We had the crib and baby carrier, "the Graco," which was the portable crib (I would say, without any real exaggeration, that I probably set up and took down that thing maybe 10,000 times over the life of our kids. I got to a point where I could do it in less than three seconds, starting with it wrapped in its case, in the dark with two crying babies, one under each arm, a diaper in my back pocket, and a bottle under my chin), the car seat, the baby books, clothes, bottles, diapers, b-pump, stroller, and you name it. We were set. Kid was even going to have his own room, which had never happened in our house.

So we did what you do when you're pregnant—we waited. We talked about names. We looked at little-kid clothes. Technology had changed quite a bit since Jessi was born, so we got sonograms that looked like photographs and shared them with friends and family. Everyone thought they were great and "cute." We were so excited. We laughed with our kids, read them stories, and talked about their little baby brother or, if God was unusually kind, a sister.

Gae had said later that things "had felt a little different." But they didn't feel different to me. We had one sonogram where the doctor said, "We are a little concerned that his legs are short and his head is large." Then he looked at me and laughed. "Nevermind. Chip off the old block. You guys are good. Enjoy, Big Head."

The day we went to the hospital, we were both giggling and laughing. Gae was in a little pain, but we had the windows down, radio on, and it was a beautiful spring day. We were doing it man, feeling and looking good. I walked into the hospital like I had just won the World Series. "Hey, what's happening? I know, 'bout to have a baby. How you feelin'?" Talking to the nurses, getting checked in, texting, and giving a couple of high fives, maybe a double finger gun or two, and then I headed up to the room. Looked like the same room Michael and Jessi were born in—3rd floor, Columbia Hospital for Women—25th and Lst NW in DC. Our midwife had just shown up. Gae was in labor. You could see the Washington Monument out our window. If the Nats were in DC at the time, they would have been in town. My parents were with our kids—they were happy. Everyone was happy. All our friends were waiting to hear the news. They were happy.

And then it broke. Our world split apart. Crashed. Car wreck. Splintered. Broken. Shattered. Speechless. Crushed. Destroyed. There is not a parent in the world that doesn't remember the first few moments of when they found out their child has disabilities like it was yesterday—the smells, the sounds, the place, the people, what you were wearing, where you were, who was speaking.

We didn't call anyone. We didn't talk to anyone. No one came over. We just sat there and held our baby and held each other. Gae said at one point, "I will raise this child, but I will never be happy again." Our lives were over.

Actually, they were just starting.

As David grew and got older, I realized that God was shaping me and teaching me in ways I had never experienced before. Hardly a day would go by where I wouldn't learn something about me, about life, and about God and Jesus through David—things about joy and peace and rhythm and courage and celebration and gratitude and suffering and surrender and what it means to be cherished and loved. So I started to write those things down and journal through them and wonder about them. And finally Gae said, "I think you need to share that. Somebody else needs to hear that."

So here it is. As best I can do. Some of my favorite stories of David coupled with my favorite stories of Jesus. I've told more than one person, the best part of the whole book are the pictures. So if that's all you do, you've probably done the best part.

www.ingramcontent.com/pod-product-compliance
Lightning Source LLC
LaVergne TN
LVHW070408070526
838199LV00016B/538